Hey, Crumbling Balcony!

Hey, Crumbling Balcony!
Poems New & Selected

Stuart Ross

MISFIT

ECW PRESS
ecwpress.com

Published by ECW PRESS
2120 Queen Street East, Suite 200, Toronto, Ontario, Canada M4E 1E2

NATIONAL LIBRARY OF CANADA CATALOGUING IN PUBLICATION DATA

Ross, Stuart, 1959 –
Hey, crumbling balcony!: poems new & selected / Stuart Ross.

ISBN 1-55022-574-X

1. Title.

PS855.O841H49 2003   C813'.54   C2002-905899-6
PR9199.3.R5993H49 2003

Editor: Michael Holmes / a misFit book
Jacket and Text Design: Dana Samuel
Jacket Illustrations: Stuart Ross
Typesetting: Dana Samuel
Production: Mary Bowness
Printing: Marc Veilleux Imprimeur

This book is set in Scala and Scala Sans

The publication of *Hey, Crumbling Balcony!* has been generously supported
by the Canada Council, the Ontario Arts Council, and the
Government of Canada   Canadä

DISTRIBUTION
CANADA: Jaguar Book Group, 100 Armstrong Avenue, Georgetown, ON L7G 5S4

ECW PRESS
ecwpress.com

CONTENTS

POEMS NEW

...I am still
The black swan of trespass on alien waters.

ERN MALLEY

The True, Sad Tale of Benjamin Peret
as It Relates to Me

Hey, balcony crumbling outside my window,
whose concrete organs plummet to the parking lot below,
know this: Benjamin Peret died in 1959
and in that year I was born.
He was photographed
in a toreador's get-up,
and thus was I born, hat and all,
waving a cape at Dr. Bernie Ludwig,
I've the pictures to prove it.

Hey, thunder of threat
that knocks the dark clouds
as if they were billiard balls
and sends poodles cowering
behind the furnace,
know this: because Benjamin Peret
croaked the year I was born,
I could not befriend him, and still
I cannot, though I try,
and I howl his name
and employ other ululations,
and I doodle his initials
on a torn piece of napkin
lodged in the throat
of an elderly neighbour
carried to the supermarket on the back of a camel
to buy six fresh eggs and a bag of prunes.

Hey, captains of industry
with your goggles and capes, your
superpowers, your considerate stationery,
I was dropped onto this planet
the year of the death
of Benjamin Peret and so
I am not his friend, nor yours,
and my mammy put me in a school for dunces
and I am a dunce, take note of my cap,
give me a dollar, a dime,
a roll of cabbage, a
piece of paper and a
reason to bespoil it.

Poem

"the cricket apparatus
is no longer
functioning. Please
insert your noise
into the bleeding
night"

Calendar Boy

He woke up.

He showered.

He was showered with Pulitzer Prizes.

Outside it was raining.

A thing got wet.

He pulled his window closed.

In his apartment,

the smell of his grandfather

who had died twenty years earlier.

He fried onions in a large pan.

The day got over.

He went to sleep.

Burial

They buried the puppy run down by the jeep.
They buried the gun that killed the teacher.
They buried the bird that fell from the sky.
They buried the mother.
They buried the father.
They buried the tangled necktie.
They buried the lightbulb that wouldn't dim.
They buried the broken blender.
They buried the capsule containing the artifacts.
They buried the frightening book.
They buried the brother who died in his sleep.
They buried the raincoat.
They buried the dollar.
They buried the songs that had long sustained them.
They buried the pen that ran out of ink.
They buried the river they'd swum in as children.
They buried Vancouver.
They buried the flower.
They buried the moustache, the beard, and the spectacles.
They buried the answers.
They buried the hatchet.
They buried the shovel and fell to their knees.

Dinnertime

A man was so big, so big
he broke all the china
in the china shop, he
made things fall over. The
bookshelves sagged. The
children sobbed. A tiny bird
whizzed out of the clouds and
perched on his ear. "Flap your
wings," the big man said,
"and carry me up to the sky."
The bird spoke no English —
it just pecked at his scalp. Dinner-
time always brought such
comfort. Tomorrow the man
would diet — no, he'd build
an electric chair. Aye,
he'd build an electric chair.

Poem of Welcome, 1953

Hello there, little green men
lined up like firewood
asleep in your capsule.
You have come far
and now must rest.
What do you eat
on your planet?
Do you have jobs?
Do your little green children
play in the streets?
Do you have streets?
Does your culture
celebrate capital?
Do you have movie stars?
If I handed you a book
would you know what it is?
If I danced for you
(and I am a superb dancer)
would you mistake my gestures
as hostile and vaporize me?
I am a man
and this place is Earth.
Have a doughnut.
Walk our roads
both paved and dirt.
Little green men, are there more
where you come from

or is your planet dead
and only you have escaped?
Do you have noses?
Do you bear gifts?
I dreamed last night that when me and Kevin
reached the top of the mountain,
he began vomiting water, convulsing.
What are you dreaming?
Do you know Kevin?
If I gave you Earth money
would you vaporize someone
I don't like?
You are little and green.
You are more famous than Abba.

Two Days Later, a Strange Quiet
Fell upon the City

I cannot sleep,
and this is why:
In front of a shoe store
where a small barefoot man
was shouting about slender red heels,
a butcher tugged at the door handle
of a station wagon lodged
in traffic. Inside the station wagon,
Georg Trakl, a German poet
who died of a cocaine overdose
in 1914, poked furiously at his cellphone,
frightened, angry,
an unpaid-for buttock of pig
gripped between his thighs.
Three minutes pass,
and more than continents shift.
O diseased world, that it
has come to this: A station wagon
speeding through side streets, a
butcher flapping like long johns
at its side, a desperate dead poet
pushing pedal to floor,
and left behind, so far away now,
shimmering like a puddle of oil
on a sun-baked highway, a

little man sobs, his white feet bare,
a pair of modestly heeled red shoes
barking at him from a wall display.
I clamp my sweaty palms over my ears
and slam my eyes shut: I can take
no more.

Frank Stella and Joe Hardy

That afternoon, Frank and Joe were arraigned before a magistrate and, after the evidence had been presented, they were held for trial on the serious charge of robbing the air mail.

"Held for the robbery!" cried Joe, aghast.

"I'm interested in simplicity rather than complexity and I think the simple thing is less difficult than the complex," declared Frank.

"Gee, Frank, this will give us a black eye all right."

"The eye can't roam around and add up relationships; there is too much going on at too high a pitch."

"Just wait till the newspapers come out. They won't do a thing but spill it all over the front page!"

"I think the general level of newspaper criticism is very low and not really interesting to anybody except as news and publicity. Magazine criticism varies a lot in quality."

"Yes, and when Aunt Gertrude hears of it she'll say 'I told you so.'"

"That's a jazz term recently used in the popular press. I don't see how it applies to painting. All painting is detached, making it a detached occupation."

Nevertheless, this did not make the situation any easier for Frank and Joe. They were in jail, and the prospect of release seemed remote.

Road Trip, Southern Ontario, 1999

We drive and drive
until we hit a lake.
At the edge of the lake
is a cairn.
The plaque reads,
"They drove and drove
until they hit a lake."
My father and I
trade glances.
A cold breeze ruffles
his thin grey hair.
Behind us,
the car idles,
the doors hanging open.
I shiver. He locks my head
in the crook of his arm.
I place my feet on his,
and he walks, giant-like,
towards the water,
carrying me with him.
"Take me to your planet,"
I say.

In the car again,
we are silent. The
sports announcer
says something about
sports. If we had been

born a century earlier,
and in Paris,
perhaps my father
and I would be walking
our turtles along the
boulevard, being silent
in French.

In two years,
my father will be dead.
The car will be mine.
Children will crack
the windshield. My feet
will touch the ground.
Oh, also, I'll have
one brother fewer. I'll have
one brother.
When the snow falls,
I will catch it
and put it back.

I Am Sitting Here

I am sitting here looking
out the window.
Someone walks by
who is not me,
doesn't even *look*
like me.

A few moments later,
another person who is
not me walks by!
What are the
chances of
that happening?

My Girlfriend's Slender Neck

After we've dated for a year,
my girlfriend reveals to me
that her neck is the neck
of a giraffe; she unwinds it
from her turtleneck collar
and I peer way up
in awe. "Are you OK
with this?" she asks. "Oh
yes," I say, "Oh yes. I
love a long and slender neck
with large brown patches.
Your neck is a sparkling
stream with lush islands
dotting its calm surface."
She smiles and wraps her neck
around me, and around me
again. "I call this the cobra
clutch," she laughs, squeezing
my torso, looking into my
eyes. "Mmm," I reply,
barely able to breathe,
my face turning the colour
of a lazy stream. I try to
smile, thinking only
of the leaves from the top
of the trees, the tastiest leaves,
the freshest leaves.

The Sun

after Georg Trakl

The sun wears the blue sky like a hospital gown.
The deer are shadows among the trees.
The man doesn't know whether to torture or nurture.

The insects skid across the pond's surface.
The earth expands and contracts.
The boat is sleepy, but it is also hungry.

Earthworms caress the corn's narrow roots.
The great mouth of night stretches wide.
A swan confronts a killer.

The planets open their moist white eyes.
The wanderer's legs are one hundred and heavy.
A flash of light tears a hole in the night.

Corrective Perjury

a parking lot
a table:

the rattling of
wooden legs
on concrete

what is on the table?
are there cars in the lot?
what price tomatoes?
is the sign in english?
how far away was the explosion?
do you like yourself?
why keep watching if it's so unpleasant?

after dark:
stillness

Laundry

The television is on, and on it
a building blows up, a man shouts
at another man, a child cowers
behind a garbage can. My father

lies in bed, and I notice, above his head,
on the wall, a lizard,
tiny and black, little more
than a crack in the plaster.

I brush it off with a rolled-up paper,
the sports section, in fact,
and it scampers across the floor
and out the door. I ask my father

if he'd like something to eat.
He shakes his head slowly, his
eyes on the television. His limbs
are thin and long

beneath the covers. I massage
his calves, then notice
another lizard, this one on
the ceiling, and another

off in the far corner. I grab
the paper and begin to swat,
but another appears on the wall,
and one on that wall. I race

about the room, swatting
at these tiny black lizards,
and every kill creates two more.

In his bed, my father breathes gently,
holds his hands up and gazes at them.

The television is suddenly silent.
My feet are off the floor and I'm
treading air. The curtains are billowing
and the lizards shuddering.

My father remembers all the things
his hands have done, these thin
frail fingers that can barely hold a ring.
They have held tens of thousands

of cigarettes, punched millions of
numbers on calculators,
pointed out hundreds of shortcuts,
caressed his wife's cheeks

and tugged on her nipples. These hands
held me high above his head,
hefted boxes from the floor,
laid levels on his workbench,
tightened vises,
wielded hammers and pliers
and trowels and paintbrushes.

He rolls his fingers slowly
in the air and turns his hands.
I drift above his bed
and he holds me high

above his head. A laugh
rumbles quietly from
his throat. I spin
in the cup of his hands.
The walls and ceiling
are dense with lizards.

This is it. This
is how it will be now.

The room is empty.

I am suspended in the centre,
tumbling like laundry.

Blind

I was coughed into the world
without eyes, though blessed
with the sockets to hug them.
As I prowled the self-conscious earth,
I thrust in different candidates:
round stones, shiny plums,
golf balls, Hostess Ding Dongs,
my own tight fists,
Florida snow globes, headlights,
newborn kittens. Each made
the landscape shift beneath
my calloused feet, but none
made a turnip taste good.

The Children of Mary Crawl Back at Night

Jesus, Mary! You've got kids!
I hear them screaming through
your apartment, I see their
toys, they look at me with
dark, dark eyes. Mary, they are
miniature people, smaller than
real ones, and they came out of
your belly. At night, when you
sleep, they crawl back in,
and there they take shelter
against the ugly things — the
cruel neighbours, the exhaust-stained snow.
And you, too, are exhausted, and so am I.
I throw a mirror in the street and try to fly.

Poem for Randy Newman's Birthday

Randy, it's exactly 6:01 p.m. and
I have begun to write your birthday poem.
I believe this one will make me a lot
of money. Randy, the first three
pop albums I bought were
Bob Dylan's *Street Legal*,
Leo Sayer's *Silverbird*, and
your *Sail Away*. Look,
I'm sorry about the Leo Sayer,
that you must be in the company
of Leo Sayer, but I liked Leo Sayer,
I like him still, and besides, who
the hell are you to talk, anyway? You
like Toto. I'm with you on Salt 'n'
Pepa, but Toto? Anyway, I've seen you,
and you squint when you sing (you probably
don't like when people draw attention
to your squint, but I like your shirts)
and I figure you have such a sharp
understanding of humans, and it's because you
squint so hard — you really, really
try to see way beyond what
others see. And now it's 6:23,
and I have spent 22 minutes
on your birthday poem. I'd better go.
Sorry about the whole Leo Sayer thing, man,
can't we just forget it?

28 November 2002

Laurie's Loss

You dropped the box, the bag,
the briefcase, the sack, you
lost the trunk, you misplaced
the shed, you forgot where you
put it, the thing, the cradle,
the armload of pages and scraps
and papers and scrawls on
napkins and transfers and gumwraps
and matchbooks. It was all that
you had and now
you are blank. You are
empty, erased. Your very big eyes
see nothing, your hands
rake surfaces, desks, seats,
beds, tables, benches, you claw
at shelves, trains, june bugs,
friends, leaves, clouds, darkness,
at words that press themselves flat
in magazines, newsrags, menus,
manifestos, books, programs, flat
against walls and ceilings, the floor.
Soon you sleep, you sleep
or lie awake, same
thing. You are without.
A bird suited cheap
in the robe of an angel,
the gown of a mental patient,
waits for the breath.
That will come.

Selecting the Proper Casket

for Owen

And the doctors are on the phone again, they are
threatening and cajoling, they have all had too much
breakfast, and we have had none, we have not
eaten, and they want to cut you to pieces
and find out what's what, but we want to put
you in the ground, into the warm arms of the ground,
we must, there is no choice, even though it's only hours
since Father heard your frightened voice and you lay
on the floor feeling your life leak from your
considerable body, and all the rules of order
were broken, and I sped through the night
in the back of a cab, rejecting all chatter,
my hands on my thighs, headlights and streetlights
blurred in my eyeballs, and soon the tiny room
filled with empty coffins, some papers shoved,
some signatures, and in your empty room
a dozen trophies gazed down at where
you should be sleeping, and we looked at the row
of uniformed boys in baseball caps
and the rabbi's voice like a kerchief flapping
and your friends pressed you into the earth
and into the earth, and my mouth is dry
against the receiver and I say, "No,"
and I sit on the foot of Father's bed
and stroke his legs as he shakes his head.

Night Sonnet

On the exercise bike, I murmur. We murmur
in the night, ice coating
the windows beside your bed.
The corned beef sandwich before you
murmurs, the coleslaw murmurs,
the secret of cabbage. The radiator
murmurs, splutters
and murmurs, we press
our hands to it; the cactus
murmurs on the window sill.
A murmur bubbles up
from the bathtub drain, and
everyone on television murmurs,
as you sleep beside me, murmuring these lines.

A Ukase for Peace

The curtain opens. A telephone
rings. A man falls over. The
sun explodes. Dogs scamper
through alleyways. The cry
of an ambulance. Emily lies
in a hospital bed. Lightning
flashes through the blinds.
The curtain falls. The audience
stir from their seats. The clatter
of heels. A scuffle. In the streets,
a cloud of snow muffles all sounds.
Throbbing cars swerve onto
sidewalks. A happy bird. A happy
bird! Billie Holiday gets back up.

Sonnet (Storm & Cat)

Toluca of California was scooped up by the wind, picked
clean off the top of a wooden fence (such as those they have
in California), her claws powerless in the ferocious blast,
and she hurled past the tops of trees, over the roof of the

Zimmermans, Bob and Roy, who were strumming their
broken guitars, and the Kabalahs, whose son was stuck down
a well in Topeka (for six years now!), and the Lemons, whose
name had been anglicized from Limón, inviting bad jokes

at every turn. Toluca looked up to the clouds that darted
through the sky like roaches, and up to the stars, and the
cats on the stars, and the chipped bowls of milk that
sat on the stars, in the stars where it was calm, where

the grass swayed lazy in a calm evening breeze,
and all was as it should be. No cats in the sky, no panic.

The Mud Above, the Sky Below

This is the year of my mother's streets,
and the streets of those with whom
she played mah jong. A snowball flies
from the fist of Bubbles the Nun,
knocks the Yiddish right out of me.
Shortly thereafter, we gather in the schvitz,
our scrawny legs poke out from towels,
and I introduce my two brothers, Horse
Race and Real Estate, who hang a versht
— a wurst — outside the door to ward off
— No, who hang a wurst outside the door
until it dries and is ready eat. Into the future
we dash, eyes peeping out between a
two and a three, those who are here for it,
those who are gone, and we leap up slowly,
into the mud,
and soon we will plummet, content,
to the sky below, and sit for our portrait
by an artist of our choice, and thus
we are prepared for war, prepared to draw
the cool cloth across our forehead,
our collective forehead, we are joined
at the forehead. We hoist our suspenders
and stroll down Coolmine, our hands
in our pockets, our eyes
in their sockets.

1 January 2003

Rescue Efforts

After everything you've seen and heard
today, you still stand your straw
in a two-ton milkshake. Look out
the frost-covered window, across
the parking lot, to the frozen creek.
That brown blur — a hedgehog. Hedgehogs
don't give a shit, not about you
or your origami leapfrogs. They slip
a quarter into the jukebox, play
"I Bereave in Love," and compare
yellow teeth. Meanwhile
you hide in the washroom,
play shootsies with a lug named Todd,
lose all your Captain Nice cards,
one by one. You cry. People cry, it's
curtains, they pump gas
into the cinema, and we tap tap tap
on the sub's lovely, talented hull.

That Which Is Not the Decoy Is Found

Long after his parents are dead,
Angry finds their wedding cake.
Not just a wedge stored for
posterity, but the whole damn thing,
with Mom and Dad — though stream-

lined — standing atop it.
A note in Dad's journal
— "the guests are fed a decoy" —
suddenly makes sense to
Angry, and Angry

lifts the top of the cake, reaches
in. There, in the safety of
the stale icing, another little
boy, this one clutching
a Johnny-7, with seven different

ways to a kill a man: 1) a bayonet;
2) a grenade; 3) a rifle; I forget
the other four, but they are all effective ways
to silence an enemy. This boy, this clutcher,
is Angry's little brother who

Angry heard so much about, or rather
nothing. Now, as sunlight filters through
the planked walls, the boys embrace,
and hamburgers appear! Magically
hamburgers appear!

Love

Mr. Sam Blatt
sewed a coat
for the dog,

his foot on the pedal,
his teeth by the sink.
We played in his room.

Mr. Sam Blatt
stood in the kitchen,
slicing up cow's tongue

and clearing his throat.
Mr. Sam Blatt
lay back in his bed,

his mouth contorted,
a pen in his hand.
He wrote Hebrew letters

on brown paper towel
and then he was dead.

Do Not Ask Where I Started

I did not ask for these feet stuck
sloppily on the ends of my legs,
the lower ends, one right, one left,
but I can see now they are useful, they
carry me and I do not tip over
while the scenery changes around me,
from street to bathroom to laundromat
to village to prison to hamburger palace,
to a great, razed field that stretches forever
with a tornado skipping through it
distant and erratic, like a frantic
spiker of refuse.
                        I was in a place
and now I am in another place.
I started somewhere and
now I am elsewhere. Rejoice.
I stand with one leg up,
and my arms — fists clenched —
bent at my sides, as landscapes
roll past like cuts of beef
on a rusty conveyor belt.
                        Soundtracks
flick by like radio stations: chanting,
recess bells, the honking of cars,
snippets of music, the yapping of
poodles, political rallies, Frank
Sinatra, Frank Sinatra, Frank Sinatra,
the whistle of wind through the

unwashed hair of a two-headed boy,
coins rattling in newspaper boxes,
false teeth jangling in plastic glasses,
the call of an egg timer, the growl
of hungry lions, the bark of orders
to a firing squad, a cake collapsing,
a lawn getting mowed.
                                   A screech of
my heels and my backdrop's a store,
and I at its counter, a gumball in one hand,
a peanut in the other, a girl with a name
on her name tag handing me coins and saying,
"You seem different from the other boys, what with
your ears, those eyes, the whole head thing
you got going, and where are you going
to?" I see her as only a brown-eyed blur,
a delicious smudge, one I could love
if someone would stop me long enough
to tell me what love is, and I say,
"I'm not going *to* nothing, I'm going
away from, that's my general direction."
And she gets all red-lipped and says, "Well,
my name is —"
                        But she's behind
me now, and I will never forget her,
the streak of brown eyes,
the feel of stuff on her I never
felt, the radiant glow of —
O, this thing of being human! These
legs! These arms! And to never

stop moving, a pinwheel nailed
to the trunk of a tree, spinning
in the breath of a breathless tornado,
whipping past the dead
whose very inertness I find so
seductive, whose deepness in the
ground, whose deepness so safe and warm,
draws me to them, or past them, past
everything, and I imagine that if I
skid to a halt, embrace
an absence of motion, perhaps
in the middle of Wilmington Park,
I could hear the blood
swim through my body, feel
the hair grow through my scalp,
more and more fingers sprout
on each hand, and I see that
I must run again, to keep me
human, to limit my fingers.
                              Hello!
My name is Underwood
manual typewriter, my name is
Ho-Ho, my name is lampshade,
my name is stuck on the snout
of a galloping weasel that
lived through the Holocaust,
my name is the name of a city
in Poland, a city in Russia, my
name is crisp salad, a new way of
fleeing, Johnny Go Darkly, a fear of

capture by creatures with claws,
by men in brown shirts, and I ask of you
this one thing:
Do not ask where I started,
I'll never remember, this is my secret, the
secret of my people, my people being me,
those of me with a foot on each leg
— one right, one left —
and a flapping verandah.

                    In the studio,
the tornado sits in a chair
across from me. "Great,"
I say, "and you've brought
a clip from your newest film, perhaps you
could set it up for us." And the tornado
sips its coffee, clears its swirling
throat, says, "Yes, I can, I will, this
scene, the one we're about to watch,
depicts me — a tornado — wreaking
havoc and chaos, you know what I mean?
I'm all about that kind of thing."
We brush our teeth, the tornado and me,
and we talk about anthrax and Sartre,
about Heidegger and Heidi Fleiss,
about the Spinners and Spinoza,
and soon the next day has come,
the sun has pushed the moon aside,
the school bell rings, and
breakfast is ready, and we —
the tornado and me — we are

chained together like Tony Curtis
and Sidney Poitier in *The Defiant Ones*.
We burst out the door
and into the street, and the tornado
sweeps me up in its arms. We
rip through the landscape,
scattering sheep, and find an apartment,
where I do the sweeping
and it cooks the chili,
and I think that this, this is finally it:
this is what I've been looking for,
the running is over, the apartment's
a mess, it's hard to keep tidy
when you love a tornado.

The Catch: Footnotes

1. Once roaches had rained down from the kitchen ceiling.

2. A flea-bitten dog sniffed at my sandals, and a boy threw a rock at it.

3. Empty, I drank coffee all night. They played a stupid movie on the plane.

4. A boy on a bicycle bumped into the curb and fell over.

5. In the 1950s, Hurricane Hazel had driven my parents into a basement.

6. Remember when the bumper cars used to come to Bathurst Manor Plaza? Aye, the bumper cars.

7. I could hear her sea monkeys laughing behind me.

POEMS SELECTED

"It is futile," I said,
"You can never —"

"You lie," he cried,
And ran on.

STEPHEN CRANE

The Adjoining Room,
or Witness to the Execution

I

The walls.
The walls of the adjoining room
were stark white.
At least
that was the first impression.
After a while
you could see they were yellowing
and smoke-stained.
And the floor?
The floor
was cold and scuffed
though no one had ever paced it.
You walked in
you sat down
you watched
you got up
you got out.

II

In the adjoining room
he sat and stared
through the window.
When at home
he stared through windows

that let him see outside
see trees
see snow —
but here he stared
at the chair
the metal hood
the ankle straps
the scratches in the arms
short white streaks
in the dark wooden surface.
And he felt the pain of slivers
ramming up fingernails
and

III

remembered a day.
Remember?
When once
walking downtown
in broad daylight
on a busy street
he was punched in the mouth
for no reason at all.
And as he sat there trembling
in the adjoining room
he remembered how he thought
at the very moment
the fist struck
how incredibly funny it was.

IV

Skull?
Shaven.

V

He made a point
of eating nothing all day
and slept a lot
the night before.
And yet
he felt lonely.
There were men and women
seated around him
they said nothing
he wanted
to speak to them
he felt
lonely.

VI

And as he sat there trembling
in the adjoining room
he remembered how he thought
at the very instant
how incredibly funny it was.
And then he stiffened
his eyes rolling back

his hair on end.
It didn't last long
and he didn't laugh once.

VII

When everyone had left
there was a shadow
in the chair.

Soldiers of Misery

after Spicer and Lorca

The banjo of the masses ascended:
"Adore me," it said,

"I am miraculous bull jelly.
Your loving rose."

Connie's trachea sounded profoundly.
"You really don't move me, Virginia."

And in Dallas, the negresses pushed their melons
into the room of misery.

Sheila's Bare Shoulders

"What kind of strata is this?"
wondered Charley,
a geology major with a girlfriend.
On his hands and knees
he ran his fingers along the rock.
Did Charley fall over
and tumble into the rock?
Yes, finally Charley fell
over and tumbled into the rock —
actually became part of the rock —
and Sheila would never see him
again.
            But in another thousand years
maybe another Charley would find him
and say, "What sort of strata is this?"
And Sheila would shrug her bare shoulders
and say, "Let's get married."
And then she'd scratch her head,
maybe remembering something.

If We Say Berlin

In churches
we agree
we don't say hell
or else that's where we'll go.
If we say Berlin
will we go there?
Will we walk the streets of Berlin
and lose our thoughts in industrial smoke
and wrap our hands around
each other's hands
and talk in whispers
like we do in churches?
In Berlin
where it is black and white
we will walk the streets
and walk the streets
and say Gezhundheit
when people sneeze
and it'll really mean something.
So what we'll do
is sneeze a lot
just so we can say
Gezundheit.
Then we'll laugh
and go to hell.

Fragments

"Fragments," he said,
"I only catch fragments."

She stabbed her steak with her fork
and met his eyes.
"How come you never listen?"

"I'm sorry," he said,
"I don't know what it is —
everything's disjointed.
Like a patchwork quilt
with the squares in the wrong places."

She threw her rum in his face
and ran from the restaurant, sobbing.

And he sat still,
trying to catch up with events.
But his mind was blank,
devoid of images
or even wiggly lines.

As the candle burned down
it came to him:
He wanted to crop his hair to the skull.

"Waiter!" he called.
"Bring shears, bring wine!"
And he tried to picture 1955.

As his hair fell to his lap
he listened to the waiter's whistling
and sipped red wine.

And with each snip
the picture became clearer.

Modern Times

This subway!
It actually *moves* —
and with me
in it.
When it stops I get out
and then I go up
moving stairs.
That's right!
An escalator!
When I reach the top
I go outside
and there are so many people
that I become one of them.
But I don't get to choose
which one I become.
Oh, life!
You're such a gamble!

Dreams of Kim Novak

Almost every night I have lousy dreams
and no one wakes me up.
The only time they wake me
is when I have dreams of Kim Novak.

The Payoff

The elephants are grateful
and dance a little cha-cha
for generous us.

Who Knows?

She sits on the subway
eating Zesty Cheese Doritos
and reading the *Enquirer*.
Maybe she killed someone today.

17 Poses: For Beginners and Advanced

I am the monster that looks up at you
from your coffee. I am Edgar Allan Poe
when you aren't looking. I cough up tiny
reptiles and free them on highways.

I am the blank image on your
turned-off TV. I am Mario Lanza
at the Alamo. I chain myself
to an ambulance and laugh at
emergencies.

I am a poet falling from a plane
into an ocean. I disappear.
I pluck out my fingernails, holding
them to the light. I am your idea
of pleasure.

I am the frozen remains of Robert
Falcon Scott. I am the sizzle
of the tainted bacon you are about
to eat. I cover my eyes
and walk through crowds.

I am the question mark above your head
as you stare, puzzled. I am someone
you once sneezed on on a bus.
I take down the Escher print
and hang myself in its place.

Soon I fall down.

In the Car

In the car
there are no flames
but around it
the world explodes

Skip and Biff
cling to the radio
the lighter
the window cranks
and feel the earth
                    shake

Skip reveals all his sins
to Biff
            and Biff confesses
that he'd always hated Skip

Around them
outside of the car
entire cities
are torn by fire
and others
are swallowed
into the earth

Soon Skip and Biff
will roll down their windows
and they will hear silence
except for crackling embers

Biff has the keys
so he'll start the car
and then they'll drive
any direction
into the sunset

E.V.M.

Exonerate my vituperative miasma.
The crowds are shirking their responsibilities.
Sirens eat at my brain, I must plug my ears.
Do you see mangled bodies climbing
the sides of respectable buildings?
They are the dead come back
to repay low-interest loans.
Quickly, we must boil eggs.
The guests are beginning to arrive.
Maybe one of them will be able to explain
that first line up there.

The Telephone Call

A man in a dark suit
enters a telephone booth.
He pulls an oyster
from his pocket,
deposits it,
and listens for the dial tone.
Jacques Cousteau answers,
says, "Life is many things —
an acrobat may hang by his teeth
but not tell his dentist."
The man in the suit hangs up,
goes to his office,
and sells his brother-in-law.

The Stupid Poems

1. NICE PEOPLE, NICE HOUSES

We are driving along Summerdale Avenue in Chicago, Illinois. Circling one particular block. The houses on Summerdale are nice houses, they are quaint, they contain nice people.

But one of the houses on Summerdale is missing. And this is the one we are interested in. We keep driving by, and slowing down, craning our heads, peering at the unkempt lawn, peering at the space where number 8213 once stood.

Other cars, too, are circling. A teenage boy hangs out a window with a Polaroid camera, his friend at the steering wheel laughing, and they circle as well. In another car, a large car, there is an entire family, and they slow down as they pass the lot where 8213 once stood. They are sort of disappointed, but they keep circling. With each orbit, another brick appears.

We are gradually rebuilding 8213. We are a chain, we circle the block, holding hands. We do not stop our cars. We do not get out and gawk. We will not walk this street. We are a big family, and we are rebuilding, rebuilding.

We stand in the dirt on the lot where 8213 once stood.
Our ankles are tangled in the weeds that have overgrown
a once-perfect lawn. A cool wind blows through our hair
and through the weeds and through our bones, and we
stare down, down into the dirt, and imagine the boys, all
the boys, the boys lying head to head, the boys lying one
on another, fucking in death, the boys with their arms
down straight at their sides, the boys with twisted faces,
with bulging eyes, the boys with torn flesh, the boys
who kept a secret for so many years.

If we are quiet enough we can hear them whisper. We
can hear their steady murmurs, the occasional laugh, as
they exchange jokes, talk baseball, talk way-out-of-date
teams. And we *are* quiet, we are so quiet, we don't
make a sound, we don't look at one another. We look
into the ground, and then we look up, at houses across
the road, and wonder what they think, those who live
there, their curtains closed, and they are quiet too, they
never speak, they don't laugh, they lie in bed at night
and think, and try not to think, and play little games till
they fall asleep.

The windows of the houses that neighbour what was once 8213 are covered with thick curtains. Each time I reach that lot I slow down, hoping to notice something new. My friends back home said I should take a shovel and a garbage bag, haul back some dirt, put it in test tubes, sell it. A surefire moneymaker, that one. "This tube certified to contain the earth that cradled the bodies of the tortured and murdered victims of John Wayne Gacy. Contents may settle during shipping." And I could sell it for $82.13 in honour of 8213 Summerdale, an address as ingrained in my mind as my own 179 Pannahill from so long ago. But there were never any bodies buried at 179 Pannahill Road, Downsview, Ontario. Not even, to my knowledge, in the sandbox up the block at Wilmington Public School.

Bunnybaby: The Child with Magnificent Ears

DR. WESTON HOLLOWAY

    Late at night, I stand here in this darkened room,

    and watch the table float in a yellow glow.

    The room is quiet but for the echo

    of the gentle breathing

    of every child who has lain upon this slab.

    I hear the tiny panting breaths,

    the first-drawn breaths,

    breaths taken through a film of bubbling mucus.

    I shiver as I make out the distinct sound,

    the fluttering gasp,

    the hoarse whisper of grating whiskers.

MR. CARLTON BOYD

    I hold no one responsible — let me make that clear.

    She feels so guilty about our little Bobby.

    She tried to keep her figure, the figure

    of her teenage years.

    The child's ears, the child's ears

    and twitching little nose.

    But soon he'll be like other boys;

    we'll forget this ever happened.

DR. HOLLOWAY

    The other day I came home

    to a lovely candlelight dinner.

    My wife emerged from the kitchen

    with a perfectly arranged platter.

A lightly broiled, marinated steak,
a mound of creamy potatoes laced with butter,
and on the side, like some cruel joke,
a Busby-Berkeley of glazed carrots.
After all I'd been through.
"You've got to get over it," she said to me.
"It's something you must overcome."
I didn't answer, just stared down the hall
and into the den,
where, on the TV screen, Bugs Bunny
was outsmarting some gullible foe.
"He's a kwazy wabbit," I told my wife.

MR. BOYD

A wildlife officer by occupation,
I deal with wild animals every day.
Often, for the safety
of the parkland-loving public,
I must order them destroyed.
But since God gave us little Bobby,
I haven't brought the hatchet down
on any creature's throat.

DR. HOLLOWAY

It wasn't just the carrots.
It was all that nuclear nonsense.
That's what I tell everyone who asks.
Maybe those carrots were tainted
is what I'm thinking.
When those two front teeth sprouted,

I did some calculations.
That nuclear accident — that explosion —
was on such-and-such a date, see;
and the conception, I figure, took place ...

MRS. HEIDI BOYD
It was those carrots.
It was magazine ads.
It was my husband.
It was TV talk shows.
It was my cravings and my foolish vanity.
When I wanted ice cream, I had a carrot.
When I wanted some chocolate, I had a carrot.
When I wanted a beer, I had a carrot.
When I felt like a side of fries,
I had a carrot.
When I craved a bowl of chili, I had a carrot.
It was those carrots.
Those carrots made my child's ears so long;
made his nose a tiny pink convergence;
gave him those teeth, that soft white fuzz.
I thank the Lord
that his body is normal,
that he doesn't want to leap the fields
and burrow deep holes in the woods.

MR. BOYD

I'm glad it was me who answered the phone.
I'll never tell Heidi about it.
The voice was thick and threatening,
and I knew right away there'd be trouble.
"Boyd, you freak bastard," this guy said to me,
"don't you make yourself sick?
You poke your thing into Mrs. Boyd
and out comes Peter Cottontail.
What have you got
inside your pants? A carrot?"
And each morning I walk into work
to a chorus of "What's up, Doc?"
and grown men twitching their noses,
their front teeth thrust over
their lower lips.
When the surgery is complete, I promised Heidi,
we will move. Our child will play with children
who will never know that once his ears
were longer than their arms.
And Heidi will make new friends
and maybe get some dental work done.
Maybe we'll find a new bridge club.
They have bridge clubs everywhere.

MRS. BOYD

Will Bobby's face be normal
when he spends his first day in school?
I walk through the mall
and in my carriage

is a dull blue blanket with two magnificent ears
reaching out like strange antennae.
It'd make a headline
right out of the tabloids:
 "Suburban Housewife Kidnaps Alien —
Raises It As Her Own Child."
But I've only got a rabbit for a son.

DR. HOLLOWAY

I no longer attend Sunday services.
Two weeks after the birth of Bobby Boyd,
Father Mulholland stopped me at the door
and put his hand on my arm.
"You have delivered the Spawn of the Beast,"
he said, and suddenly I had the vision
of Bobby's newborn gleaming face
staring blindly at me from the blankets,
his downy forehead drenched with a river of illness.
And little Bobby said to me,
"Dr. Holloway, there can be no blame."

MRS. BOYD

Maybe I'm special.
Carlton has said this so often.
Maybe the Lord, in His wisdom and glory,
placed me on this earth
to bring Bobby to His kingdom.
Heidi Boyd will show that all creatures are equal.
God is indifferent to species —

elephant, antelope, weasel or kangaroo.
Bobby exists to blur the lines,
to spread the love of God.

DR. HOLLOWAY

And me so close to retirement.
It's odd that Bobby should happen to me now.
It's like a warning:
"Never relax.
Never let your guard down."
Maybe when I'm ninety
a spacecraft will land in my backyard.
Little Bobby, bless his buck teeth,
is a signal to me, a light.
"Never relax.
There may be surprises."

BOBBY BOYD

My ears are twin towers of Babel.
My whiskers are numbered
and each contains a sin.
The twitching of my pink nostrils
is the history of all the earth.
My two front teeth
are my parents, Adam and Eve.
I am Bunnybaby. I am Bugs
and I am Brer. I am Peter Cottontail.
I am every rabbit shot and wounded,
twitching bloody in a field,
waiting for the kiss of God.

I am a child's mask
on Hallowe'en. I am my mother's
worst nightmare.
I am Everyrabbit.
Come hop with me.
Come hop with me.
Come hop with me.

Yikes!

My nose!
it's in the garbage!
and everything's oozing
from this hole
in my face.

Three Scoops, Waffle Cone

When they took inventory
in hell
Velda thought maybe
Garrett
had took
some paper clips.

Ladies & Gentlemen, Mr. Ron Padgett

I. LADIES & GENTLEMEN, MR. RON PADGETT

Sitting there late at night
in the empty subway car, Ron,
I was reading your stuff,
reading *100,000*
Fleeing Hilda, reading
Bean Spasms, reading
the translations,
Triangles in the Afternoon, *Toujours L'Amour*,
reading *Tulsa Kid*.
Ron, I read
Great Balls of Fire.

And it depressed me in the end,
because I wished I
had written all that,
and I began to sweat,
fell to my knees,
and dashed my head
on the subway floor.
"Damn!" Thud! "Damn!" Thud! "Damn!"

II. FIVE GUYS NAMED RON

This one'll be sort of exploratory, Ron.
Let's see who else we know with your name.

1)   Ron Justein, who I met in first year;
     everyone thought we looked identical.
     We were sort of friends, but it was forced.
     People'd come up to me:
     "Hey, Ron, how'd you do in the football pool?"
     I could've said something witty, like "Drowned,"
     but I just said, "I'm not Ron."
     Then I'd smile sheepishly so they wouldn't feel stupid.
     Did Ron go through the same thing?

2)   Ron Stewart — he was a hockey player back
     when I watched. I watched because it was on
     after *My Favorite Martian*
     and because I liked Dave Keon
     and I liked watching the rink wall open up
     when players went into the penalty box.
     Much later, Ron Stewart was somehow involved
     in the death of Terry Sawchuck, I think —
     but I'll look it up before this gets published
     so I don't get sued.
     Notice how his name is almost a blend of ours.

3) Ron Mandelson, my oldest brother's friend from
the Bathurst Manor days. He had a brother
named Larry and he wore glasses
and had unbelievably huge sideburns.
Rather a minor figure in literature, I think.

4) Ron Ross is my cousin in Los Angeles.
Although I call him Ronnie, others
call him Ron, so here he is.
Like Ron Mandelson, he has a brother
named Larry. I've met Ron once,
maybe twice, he was a nice guy,
we played cards.

5) Ever hear of the movie star Ron Ely?
Blond, blue eyes, and always seemed
a bit too old. He played Tarzan,
might've been his first film, and then
he took over the Miss America
or Miss World or Miss Universe
or something Pageant. Pageant?
Why, that's like Padgett!
A lousy actor
brings us full circle.

Ron, you know how us poets
keep little notes
scrawled on just about everything
with little phrases we think up
and might someday use?
Like, you go into a store
to buy a pack of gum
and reach into your pocket
for a one
and you come out with a piece of paper
so worn
you thought it was money,
but it ends up being one of those "idea phrases"
you just wrote down
in pencil
and now it's fading
and soon it'll be gone
and if it was any good you'll never know.
Anyways, Ron, the point is,
I have one of those
little phrases
and it's been years
and I still haven't used it.
Maybe it's no good, I don't know,
but why don't you have it —
use it if you want:
"Death creep, be my baby."
No, really, go ahead,
take it.

IV. PROGRESS REPORT

How's it going so far, Ron?
Have you read up to this one?
Do you like it?
Do you think I'm a jerk?
Do you hate my guts?
Or did the copy I sent you
get lost in the mail?

V. RIDING INTO TULSA

Tulsa is a city
in the United States,
in Oklahoma to be exact.
How many people can you name
who hail from Tulsa, Oklahoma?
How about Mr. Ron Padgett?
The poet?
Yes, Mr. Ron Padgett the poet.
But, of course —
he is from that fine state
of Oklahoma.

Mr. Ron Padgett from Tulsa, Oklahoma,
born 1942. During the war.
We do not know the extent
of its influence on his life.
Ron remembers John F. Kennedy's death.
Remembers Robert Kennedy's death.

Remembers Harvey Milk's death.
But don't spread rumours —
Ron has a wife and son.
But he knows Kenward Elmslie.
But heterosexuals and gays
can be friends
like anyone else, don't worry.
I wasn't worrying, I was just saying
maybe the wife and kid are a cover.
But what difference would that make?
None whatsoever.

Ron writes, Ron teaches,
and Ron translates. Sometimes
I think maybe he's more academic
than he lets on.
You think he's serious?
Serious, yes. But serious, I think,
about being goofy.

People from Tulsa are generally serious.
Is that so?
Yes, Tulsa is a serious place.

VI. COUNTING ON RON

I don't like what I see
south of the border, Ron.
I know there's already
a lot of pressure on you,

being a poet and all,
teaching at colleges,
running St. Mark's,
turning in the new manuscripts on time, etc.,
but I want to know I can count on you
to do what you can
to work things out.

to, do, what, you, can,
to, work, things, out.

What a lousy bunch of words, Ron,
not an image among them.
I'm really sorry.
I've buggered things up, haven't I?

You're on to me now,
you know I'm slumming,
you figure I'm writing letters,
not poems.

STAND UP, RON!
REACH ACROSS THE BORDER
AND GIVE ME A GOOD
SLAP IN THE FACE!

That'll teach me.
That'll teach me good.

VII. GIVING RON THE BUSINESS

We've never met,
me and Ron.
Just thought I'd throw this in
so people don't get the wrong idea,
like that we're chums
from way back when.

I'm not saying we've never met,
because maybe once
it was Ron who asked me directions,
or Ron who stepped on my toe on the bus.
If he's been to Toronto it's possible,
because I *do* get around.

Okay, let's pretend
I'm meeting Ron.
We'll meet at Toby's Hamburgers
by the corner of my street.
"Hi, Ron, is this okay?"
"Sure, Stu, but let's move to smoking."
"Oh, Ron, I didn't know."

Then the waitress comes up.
She knows me since I'm there a lot.
"This is my friend Ron.
I wrote a book about him
and he called me up
and now since he came to visit Toronto

we're getting together."
The waitress nods.
"He's a poet," I continue. "Pretty
big in the States. There was a whole issue
of *Strange Faeces*
devoted just to him. He's collaborated with
Joe Brainard and Ted Berrigan and Jim Dine and Tom Veitch."
The waitress says, "What about Tom Clark?"
"Tom Clark?" I say. "That one I don't really know.
You'll have to ask him yourself.
What about it, Ron?"

But Ron's not really there,
it's just hypothetical.
We'd sit,
and I'd razz him,
and slap him on the shoulder,
give him the business
about the whole American scene.
I'd say "heh-heh"
when I was facetious,
so as not to offend him.
Those Americans're touchy, you know.

Ron would have The Popularity,
which has mushrooms,
I'd get The Truckstop,
your basic banquet burger.
He'd offer to pay,
then I'd say, "No,

let me take it,"
and then find I left my wallet at home.

The waitress would say,
"Don't worry about it.
This is Mr. Ron Padgett."

And everyone'd turn their heads.

Wait for the Rattle

You who have scotch-taped your feet to the floor
and secured all movable objects in your household
You who have put velcro upon your dog and
fastened her to the wall with her water dish near
You who have stashed canned foods and liquids
and taken care of all loose ends
You who have disconnected all electrical equipment
and forwarded your mail to no fixed address
All of you
Listen:

On the shelf in your kitchen
there is a coffee cup
or maybe a tea cup
It sits motionless like a skull in a desert
Keep your eyes glued to that cup
think about that cup
that one thing

Wait for the rattle

The Laundry Boy

The laundry boy folds
the laundry
fresh from the dryer
folds those sheets
over and over
folds them till
they fit in his pocket
then takes off his pants
and folds them too
till they fit in his mouth
then grabs the washer
and the dryer and folds them
and puts them in his cart
steps out of the laundromat
and folds it too
and puts it in the adjacent restaurant
then folds it too
and folds up the whole block
all the stores
the newspaper boxes
the stray dogs
the lampposts
and puts them in his little cart
and putters along the street

He is just a little dot
and the city is so big

Paralysis Beach

I

From a bridge not far
away I watch
those heavy figures
at water's edge.
They are bending, perhaps,
to examine a shell, or
a bottle cap, an ice cream wrapper,
a broken umbrella, a severed
digit, an awkward turnstile,
a limping factory,
a burning candle of ecstasy.

II

The hot-dog stand
is very far away.
Hank stands there humming,
holding a knife,
hand suspended
over the mustard. The mustard
is good, the buns
are good, Hank
is patient. He feels, deep down,
that soon,

very soon,
he'll be visited.
Maybe a fat lady
in sunglasses, maybe
the Pope.

III

A communist named Norm
has an insect up his nose,
cannot find the hot-dog stand,
has a bottle cap impacted
in his foot, is
scared of water, suspects
his wife of infidelities
as he wanders the beach,
twitching.
A ghost hovers over Norm,
panting his name
on a frequency
heard only
by surfers.

IV

The hollow restaurant
is starting to decay. It's
a Family Sort of Place.
A former journalist
waits on tables,
bursts, hair on end,
into the thick kitchen heat:
MAN, 43, WANTS SOUP,
SEEKS SIDE OF FRIES.
The chef nods, butts out
his cigarette, kicks off
his shoes, scratches his ass,
and lifts the ladle from the floor.

V

In dead night,
I peer through smoke-stained windows,
watch the tiny distant flashes
beyond Paralysis Beach. Lord,
I have a tuba in one hand,
a deck of cards in the other.
I crawl to the bed, press
a damp pillow over my head.

VI

Norm's the first
this morning. The beach
is his.
He scurries to the rocks,
leaps into shadow.
Norm is carrying every newspaper
in the whole world, knows that way
he'll find what he wants.
From those suffering rocks,
he sees the beach twitch,
small eruptions blistering
the haggard surface. Tiny
amphibious creatures bubble up
and Norm knows them all by name.
"Here, here, here,"
mutters Norm, peeling off
his shirt.

The air shudders above him,
chills run through
him, the surfers
are coming in.

VII

Old women
coat the walls
of the billiards room, cawing.
They apply chalk
to their eyelids and
lips, fling the blue cubes
at old men
who circle the tables
again and again, hefting
their warped cues, choking
on clouds of talc, spitting
into the pockets.

Hank watches from
behind smoked glass, learns
all the tricks, waits for the day
when he, too, is old,
when his throat sags
and his vision blurs,
and he can put the brown
in the far left pocket,
startling
a sleeping rat.

VIII

Far out,
beyond the water's edge,
a small girl's head
is tugged below.
Her name is Anna, she excels
in finger-painting, is a hit
among the boys, can spell
real well, wants a pet cat,
is six years old. Anna
enters another world,
her lungs fill with water,
her mother tans
beyond recognition.

Eddie is the lifeguard, his flesh
sags over the chair, his eyeballs are crushed
to his sunglass lenses. Eddie
is a favourite, too; the girls
cluster to him, listen to
his wheezing, bubbly breath,
they touch his arms, his chest.
"Do you like baloney?
Where you from?" They
invite him to parties, to
seances, to
church picnics, to
back seats of cars. Eddie
just wheezes, his torso rumbles,

he drools, mouth begins to open,
girls silent, Anna has no gills,
Eddie clutches his belly,
folds over, shudders,
says,
"I was born hard."

IX

Gather round me, God's children,
Take a bullet in your teeth,
The subway's a-comin',
Don't get tangled beneath.

Gathered under
rainbow umbrellas,
the choir pounds
the shimmering
gospel heat.

Ill vipers burst
from the shadowed sand,
tiny teeth flashing
into fleshy ankles.
As the choir sings, a child
scampers from foot to foot,
fighting the vipers
with a plastic shovel.
Above, way above,
where the voices don't reach,

a dark plane trails
a long plastic banner:
BUY DISMAL ITEMS.

The gospel women swoon,
tear their mouths still wider,
their large robed bodies
trembling with sweat.

X

When swollen moon
eats through the sky,
I push my legs to briny edge
and comb the foam for remains.

XI

They ride
the very tip
of waves
that move
like molasses.
Every morning they appear
on the watery horizon, each day
their slow
and painful journey
fails to reach
the beach. The sun
sinks in torment, they start

to fade, their ears are filled
with the roar of water
and the whisper of a ghost
hissing, "Norm, Norm, Norm,
Norm, Norm ..."

XII

The kid with the radio
blaring country & western's
got a lobster hanging
from each ear.
His chest is sunken,
his mother cuts his hair,
his sandals keep slipping,
his neck is fried red.
"I ain't got no father,"
he says to the sand,
and he's heading for the restaurant,
right past Hank,
yeah, the Carter Family singing,
Chef's Special on his mind.

XIII

Buried on the beach
beneath sand and debris,
I borrow language
from passing insects, the sun
bakes my hair white.
Children approach me,
bite off my protruding toes.

No one will buy me
an ice cream today.

Tengo Fuego

I have fire, I have
a light, I got a
match, right here
in my shirt pocket, right —
Shit, it's gone,
my shirt is gone,
I groped my own breast.
Looking for a match
to light this cigarette
dangling from my lips
I groped *me*. Yee-ha.
Nobody noticed.
They went on sipping their
coffees, talking about Truffaut
and Derrida, about
elves and elks, about British
miners, about nice boys.
A girl with glasses, she looks
real smart, just looked
in my direction, yee-ha.
She's smoking, I run my fingers
through her tangled hair —
in my *dreams*, I do!
Yee-ha. I'm an eel,
a cigar, a banana,
a cannon. I'm tiny
and I climb up the side
of my coffee mug and tumble

in. Yikes! Someone help me!
I wave my little armitos
but no one sees me.
I have become a common housefly
drowning in my own coffee,
coffee that *I* paid for —
imagine that!
The girl with glasses is
getting up, she's putting on
her jacket, she's walking out
the door. I am helpless. My wings
are drenched.
I sink to the bottom
of the mug. I lie there
and try to buzz.
I remember my dog.
He will be sitting by his dish
waiting for food.
Waiting for me
to come and feed him.
But I've become a drowned fly
and I will not come home
to feed my dog.
Poor little
droopy-eyed thing.

Little Black Train

Waiter there's an alligator in my eye
and christ I need a shave
the way people look at me
I mean I know I'm pale
got these rings under my eyes
my whole face is tense
looks like I haven't slept for a week
but I have
really

I'm waiting for something
but every time I look at my watch
to see if it's late
I have no watch
and my bare wrist winks up at me
sends me a kiss
says Buy me a watch big boy
make me pretty
like all the other wrists

Pretend I'm rich real rich
I have a heated swimming pool right in my living room
hard to believe but it's true
I walk up to the edge
and drop all my clothes
right there in my living room
outside it's snowing

I can see through my huge picture window
through which my neighbours all watch me
in awe
Look at him honey they say
a picture of splendour
and right in his own living room

I jump in
and the water doesn't even ripple
doesn't splash onto the carpet
and then I'm under
gliding along the bottom of the pool in my living room
back and forth
around and around
doing these little acrobatic flips when I get to each end
I don't need to come up for air for oh five minutes or so
and when I do
I see there's a crowd at my window
and before I go under again
I hear them yell Jump Jump Jump
and I realize jesus I'm not in a swimming pool
I'm on the ledge of a ten-storey building
a ten-storey building right in my own living room
and below way the hell down there
there's so much traffic
and it's raining
and I see my grade six teacher Mrs Sibbald walk by
Mrs Sibbald I call Mrs Sibbald
and she stops and looks up and puts her hand to her mouth

I remember you she yells
over the din of the honking horns
and my neighbours calling Jump Jump Jump
You were a clever boy she yells
but you didn't have a mind for science
do you still see that Sidney Radomsky
I once saw a cloud that looked like his shape I yell back

My doorbell rings
and it is the postman of course
Mister do you know it's nearly two in the morning I say
and he hands me a box tied with string
and says Sign here
and says You look like you could use a little sleep
and I sign
and I say Yeah well here you are coming here at 2 a.m.
and I close the door and untie the box and lift the lid
and this boxing glove pops out
and punches me right in the nose
and I open the box again
and this boxing glove pops out
and punches me right in the nose
and I open the box again
and this boxing glove pops out
and punches me right in the nose
This is it I say
This is the human condition
this is what it all boils down to
this is the bread and butter

this is the nuts and bolts
this is the crime and punishment
this is the Tom and Jerry

And there's a pounding on the wall
that shakes the ashtray on my head
and my neighbour's voice at two in the morning
People trying to sleep in here
people got jobs you know
I go to the wall and pound with my fist
How the fuck do you expect to sleep
if you're yelling and pounding on the wall
But we love each other my neighbour and I
and his children Mary Astor and Dick Powell
named after movie stars you are too young to remember
and tomorrow all will be forgotten
and we will lend each other power tools
and he will ask me why I have an ashtray on my head

Oh wait I lied back there I *am* wearing a watch
well I didn't really lie
but it slid so far up my arm
that I just found it now
just found it through my shirt
while I was feeling how my biceps were doing
and thinking about Russian literature
I mean I don't get much exercise
there's no denying that
I'm not trying to hide anything or steer you wrong
I plead guilty before the court of physical fitness

but I was thinking about Popeye
and I was checking out my biceps
and there it was like a miracle
like the parting of the Red Sea
like Jesus met the woman at the well
my watch
right there up on my biceps
and you could have fooled me
I really had no idea
it's four in the afternoon
and we have nothing at all to do
and I think Dick Van Dyke is on
pull up a chair
while I go shave

The Uneven Century

"He paces the blue rug. It is the end of summer,
the end of his excursions in the sun."
                    Frank O'Hara

As if everything were final.
As if they had never invented erasers.
As if the bridges were burned behind him.
As if there were no memory.
As if the cake had caved in.
As if the cake had caved in.
As if there were no soap, no rug shampoo, no disinfectant.
As if you couldn't change your mind.
As if ice wouldn't melt.
As if they couldn't ever be friends again.

Glurb dnuson vleed,
cragga resnap cletch.

City of My Dreams

I find myself attracted
to the desolation of monogamy.
Although it tears at my heart
to see those who are stuck there
through no choice of their own,
it strikes for me a chord of belonging.
I feel at home in its decay.
I rest in its crumbling churches.
I am charmed by its broken telephones,
crossed wires, bad connections.
My own sense of directionlessness
is mapped out on its nameless streets.

Wait! Did I say monogamy?
I meant Managua.

Cottage Country

A cloud plummets.
The screen door swings open.
On the stove a cheese sandwich burns.
This is my religion.
Barry climbs through the window.
He smells of insect repellent.
His arms glisten.
A rusted fishhook juts out
from the dock's soft wood.
There is sand between my toes.
A boy hits another boy.
The container with the catfish
lies on its side.
The fish is gone. It is just a container.
A car won't start.
The brothers no longer speak.
Their wives meet clandestinely.
A famous boxer arrives.
Celebration.

Reconsidering Things

I would like to go for a walk
a nature walk
you know, through woods and stuff
along rivers
stop and look at insects
listen to all the different birds
follow trails
where spiderwebs get in your face
lizards flee your approaching step
and maybe there's a horse just standing there
just standing there
among the trees
like he's waiting for a bus
his tail swinging at flies —
or a bear!
I could see a bear!
holy, I'd run so fast
I'd drop my copy of *Walden*
and my bag of sandwiches
and the bear'd pick them up
split the food with the horse
and trade *Walden*
to the lizards
for a copy of Blake

The Clamour

Was like a little Nosferatu
village, everybody running around
with coffins tucked
beneath their arms,
scurrying and seething
in fast motion
like frames were missing
between their movements.
Maybe some kind of
crazed ant colony, you blink
and suddenly there's twice the insects
climbing over one another,
moving in barely recognizable
chains, with brains
so small they feared not
the big foot. Lisa turned
to me and said, "Call me
Lisa," and I was just agape.
"How can you even think
of that at a time
like this! We're in some kind
of emergency!"
We huddled in the doorway
of an abandoned shoe store
and the din was so dense
you could cut it with maybe
a petrified ear, but a normal
ear, all fleshy and soft —

no way. A man held a long stick
high above the crowd, a
poodle tied to it, blindfolded,
a ribbon in each ear. "I've got
my own problems without
all this shit," I told Lisa.
She put her hand to my
brow and told me I had a
fever, to calm down, to
go with the flow. A flailing
woman just then was passed
over the heads of the rampaging
mob, and I nearly swallowed
my teeth. "I once loved her!" I called,
pointing. "Or someone just like her!"
Feeling suddenly dizzy, I sunk
to the ground, and the roar
and the wheeze and the
crash of the crowd
churned in my stomach
and my gut was a lost sailor
in a black raincoat
and a four-day beard,
slashing at an entire
raging ocean
with a weather-beaten oar
and curses
the size of
the whole grinning
sky.

What He Thought When He Thought

In the great empty dancehall
of his skull,
she moves like a cartoon,
her face a threat,
her small fists swinging,
her black shoes skidding across the floor.
He stands in a corner talking,
and he keeps talking,
his mouth keeps moving,
he finds himself talking,
he can do nothing but talk,
and his voice is the broken buzzer
of an oven timer.
He looks down, finds
a window in his chest,
and he peers in
and sees himself standing
in the corner of a crowded ballroom,
and then she appears
and she moves like a cartoon,
a cyclone,
her fists thrashing,
her black shoes skidding across the floor.

1993

Radio sizzling between stations
in the next apartment
Candle wax splattered across the table
Here: scrape the tears from your face with this
Kick off your shoes
Throw everything into the pot
while the fire's going
One of these days you open the window
& it smells like Managua
or wherever you dream of
Some boll weevils reading
Faulkner on the curb &
though the wind has called it a day
the tire in the tree keeps swinging
Yeah well
i'm lying on the floor
humming labour songs
& someone's coming
to fix something

Sonnet

Based on the 1960 movie *Strangers When We Meet*
starring Kirk Douglas and Kim Novak.
Based on the lie the guy told his child
in the seat behind me on the streetcar.
Based on the way the moonlight
filtered through her curtains
the night her brother was killed by a car.
Based on a half-forgotten song I heard in Holland.
Based on how he loved her,
then hated her, then loved her.
Based on the shape of an unearthed skull.
Based on the idea
there's a heaven and hell.
Based on that night at the King Slumber Motel.

Señor Cuerpo

This is what I did:
I went to sleep
and when I woke,
my fists,
clenched in nightmare,
were dying armadillos,
my arms were rotting carrots
wrapped around my torso,
a bag of stinking laundry.
I flung back my bedsheets
and peered down my legs:
the left was a bundle of barbed wire,
the right an expired parking meter.
My feet, which gleamed in the morning sun
that streamed through my window
like a river of hope,
were waffles. Burnt waffles
drenched in syrup.
Yeah, I know what you're wondering —
it was a salt shaker now,
nearly empty.
I turned and peered
into my bedside mirror.
My head was intact.
Imagine.
Though my face was never
a thing of beauty,
there it was: my face.

My ears were ears,
my mouth had lips,
my eyes were glazed,
my hair still hair.
I lay back and stared
at the ceiling.
I thought about my life.
The house I grew up in.
The schools I attended.
My mother, my father, my brothers.
My grandparents, now dead, all four.
I thought about
the books I had read
and the paintings I'd seen.
I thought about what I'd eaten last,
and what I'd said,
and what I'd thought.
I'd have thought about what
I'd had to drink,
but I hadn't drunk.
You've got to believe me.
I dressed myself
as best I could,
held my face under running water.
I grabbed my briefcase
and ran for the bus.
At the office my In-tray
was piled higher than a Dagwood,
my phone didn't stop ringing,
my boss leaned on me and wept.

In spite of my
physical awkwardness
I was incredible.
By the time I left
I'd been promoted three times
and had married the president's daughter.
But none of this made me happy.
I took six months' leave
and travelled to a country
that didn't know English.
I consumed only liquid
and studied the saxophone,
teaching the armadillos at the ends of my carrots
a thing or two about fingering.
I tapped my burnt waffles
like some veteran hepcat,
drawing great gusts of breath
from the depths of my laundry.
My music howled through the nights,
through bars and clubs,
through taxis and trucks,
through darkened homes.
I played that music,
music that leapt
from the decaying junkyard,
the fermenting forest
that was my body,
and I played till I collapsed,
every night till I collapsed,
and sunk to the bottom

of a sleep I hoped
might make my body whole.
But each morning it was the same:
the carrots, barbed wire,
waffles and parking meter,
the salt shaker, the laundry,
the armadillos.
And in the hour of the exhausted scream,
when the sun stuck a toe in the sky,
when newspapers were still blank sheets
and the dead returned to their coffins,
I hunkered down on my four strange limbs
and clambered through the empty streets,
pushing, pushing that body,
pressing my face
to the cold, cold concrete.

Frank Poem #1

It's my lunch hour, so I go
down seven floors
to the cafeteria
and Norma tells me for the hundredth time
that I remind her of her son,
although he is a hulking creature
maybe twenty times my size.
Dave is wearing the same T-shirt,
says "I'm still asleep." I laugh,
hoping it will get me
a bigger portion.
And as I approach the cash
where Sam is smiling sadly (his business
is flocking across the road, where the food
is better, the plates are real),
I see the woman from the third floor
lining up to pay. I step forward and
lift a finger to the air. I say,
"Woman from the third floor,
we both work in this office building,
though for different companies,
but we find ourselves approaching
the same cashier so often. Is this alone
not reason for love?
Our destinies are entwined like ...
What if I gave you an original Breughel ...
Do you like to shoot snooker, I know a place ...
Just ride the elevator with me ...

You get off at three and I at seven.
No, not o'clock,
I was referring to floors."
Alas! This office building thing
is not for me!

I Have Something to Tell You

I've come to talk to you about shaving cuts
I was waiting across the road
right over there
for the light to turn
and you were on the other side
fumbling with change at the newspaper box
don't buy this one buy this one
I said
pointing to identical newspapers
look here
I cut myself shaving
and both my hands are cameras
do you think that's why I can't hold a razor
my feet too are cameras
and my belly
made round by beer
that's a camera too
a big camera
each of my eyes
they're cameras
they work good in the dark
and my mouth
well it's not a camera
but when it opens
out comes my tongue
an actual camera
some people have cameras mounted on each shoulder
but each of my shoulders

is a camera
or each *are* a camera
grammar not being my strong suit
and speaking of suits
look what I done to this one this morning
I was shaving
dad said shave before you get dressed
right after you shower
while your face is soft
but always the rebel
I showered got dressed *then* shaved
and look what I've done to my suit
of course it's hard holding razors
no matter how soft your face is
when your hands are cameras
have I told you about my hands

Sitting by the Judas Hole

They rip the door off its hinges,
dash it to the floor.
They say, Now you can leave.

I walk out onto the porch,
squint against the sun.
There's a man in a cap
at the edge of my lawn,
his arm rotates like a windmill,
faster and faster,
I hear it whistling.
I know him somehow
from many years back.
He yells,
"I'm not on your property,
I'm on the road!"

His jaw slides up and down
and I wonder, Is this guy
a puppet?
Or is he dubbed?
His words don't match
his mouth.

But forget the mouth,
the pinwheel arm is a blur,
a Ferris wheel out of control.
Children are screaming,
clutching each other in fear.

And then it is still. The arm
is still. But I can still
hear a whistling — not the
whistle of the arm. The arm
is still.
Something else appears.
It gets bigger and bigger.

"I'm not on your property,
I'm on the road!"
Yeah, but I saw his foot on the curb,
the curb's my property.

And they say, The curb belongs to the city.

But the curb's my property. My property
ends at the curb, but includes
the curb. The curb —

Something slams into
the bridge of my nose, I want
to vomit, I stumble back,
right back into my house, and
through tear-filled eyes I see a ball
rolling off the porch, a baseball.
It comes to a stop on my lawn.

The front of my shirt is bloodied.
I am aghast — I've just had it dry-cleaned.
I have the receipt to prove it.
Please replace my door.

* * *

I sit in a chair
facing the closed door.
My forehead leans beneath
the Judas hole.
I hear footsteps on my porch.
Sir Robert Falcon Scott.
I loved Sir Robert Falcon Scott.
John Dillinger.
I loved John Dillinger. He did not die.
Montgomery Clift.
I loved Montgomery Clift.
I loved his eyes,
the way they watered.
He did not die.
Sir Robert Falcon Scott
is very cold.
I shiver.
My ankles are bound
in plastic cord;
I cannot dance.
The cord snakes through
the legs of the chair,
down the hallway,
through the kitchen,
and into another hallway beyond,
to my telephone.
The cord is attached to the telephone.
If the telephone rings I'll scream.
The telephone is the monster

that carries her voice, carries all
their voices. I remember her voice.
Her voice is the sound of my heart
thudding to a stop,
falling flat on its face.
My heart is a cartoon.
It is projected on the wall.
It is a beached whale;
it wheezes in the sand.
I'd like you to meet my heart.

* * *

You shiver, your forehead
rattling against the door.
The faintest sound of scratching
reaches your ears.
And little plops, you think
you hear little plops,
the sound of lizards hitting the floor.
Above your head,
someone is peering in.
Isn't that the rustling of eyelashes?
Isn't that the twang
of legs stretching?
Something brushes against your foot
and you convulse. You jerk your feet
from the floor,
place them on a rung of the chair.
"Lizards," you say.

"Lizards."
If greenbeans had legs
and two beady eyes, and
if greenbeans could scurry
and flick their tongues,
then greenbeans would be lizards.
With lizards falling from the walls
and strangers peeping through the door,
you change your tune.
"Greenbeans," you say.
"Greenbeans."
After a few hours
you've become dogmatic —
that is to say,
you've become your own best friend.

* * *

This is certain:
somewhere someone
was once in love.
Murmurs curled through the thick smoke
of candles. Ankles were entwined.
In the dark sky, glimpses of a setting
sun were caught between mountains
of orange cloud. There was breath on a neck.
A hair on a pillow.

Now there is the roar
of the city, the squealing

of tires, the howling of dogs
fucking in busy intersections,
the slam of elevators at every floor,
the deafening rattle of streetcars
delivering corpses.

Step into a bakery.
Buy bread and eat it.
Tear it with your teeth.
Buy yourself a paper bag
and put something in it.
Then buy a newspaper,
throw it in the air.
See how it lands in the hands
of those who want it?
Rent a car.
Drive it into a ravine.

I hear a whisper follow me. I run
around a corner and catch my breath.

* * *

A piece of paper slides under
the door. It hits my toes.
I open my clenched-shut eyes.
Blobs of colour float around
my field of vision,
till finally I can
make out the writing on

the flyer. It says Chinese
Food, it says Tea Leaf Readings,
it says Half-Price Snowtires, it says
Hot Dogs All-Dressed. It says a
neighbourhood committee is being formed
to catch the second-floor rapist, it says
my Conservative member of parliament
is doing a cracker job, it says
recycling boxes will be distributed
to Every Fucking Household.

Each letter is cut
from a different source
and pasted down haphazardly.
It says We HavE YOuR chILd,
WE wANt yoUr MOneY,
wE Buy aLL yoUR cARRotS,
we Like YOUr haiRCUt.

I dangle one arm
like a worm on a hook
and pick up the paper.
I turn it over. I
read it. The blobs are
gone from my eyes, I can
read now. It says,
"I'm standing here
this side of the door.
I'm waiting for you.
I'm as bad as you remember.

Please open up. I love you."
The handwriting is familiar.
It belongs to everyone
I've ever known.
They took turns, one letter
each, an exquisite corpse,
a chain of fools, dominoes made
of razor blades.

It's good for a laugh. I
unfold the paper.
It is a note from my landlord.
I've missed my rent.
He wonders how many bodies I've
buried under the floorboards.
He is eager to excavate.
He will find nothing.
There is nothing to find.

I'm crazy with love
but I keep forgetting.

* * *

I would like to talk about death now.
Did you see the puddles in the grave?
Did you see the gravediggers nearby,
heads hanging, hands folded?
Did you see the shovels jammed in the dirt?
Did you see the pallbearers' faces?

Did you see the rust on the sides of the hearse?
Did you hear the rabbi's voice shake?
Did you hear the son's voice shake?
Did you hear the bus drive by while they lowered the coffin?
Did you see the ad on the side of the bus?
Did you read the ad?
Do you remember the product?
Will you buy some?
Will you buy *me* some?

* * *

They say:
The guests will begin arriving
in forty-five minutes. You've got
to remove your head from the door
and pull yourself together.

I say:
I didn't call this party.
There are lizards on my wall.

They say:
Have you prepared the hors d'oeuvres?
They'll expect little sandwiches,
bowls of nuts, glasses of wine,
vegetables and dip. They'll expect
a smile on your face. They'll expect
music. Music for dancing. Dance
music.

I say:
My body is a lead weight.
I cannot move. Lizards
crawl about my shoulders and neck.
I'm too tired even
to shudder in revulsion. I'm afraid
I'm unable
to entertain right now.

They say:
But can't you hear them?
They are preparing to leave,
buttoning their shirts,
knotting their ties,
rolling on their nylons,
clearing their throats,
climbing into their cars.
They have pieces of tissue
stuck to their shaving cuts.

I say:
Hey! Somebody put something
in my cyanide!

* * *

My enemy has held his grudge for far too long.
The grudge is the size of a croquet ball,
and wet and yielding as clay.
He holds the grudge in his hands,

rotating it, staring into it.

Each day it becomes smaller and harder.

It becomes more precise.

It burns his hands

and he turns it more quickly.

He can see to the very centre

of the grudge in his hands,

he can see its heart,

the heart's teeth clenched.

When I pass my enemy in the street,

he tucks his grudge in his coat

and sneers. I am stoic. Calm.

His hatred singes my sideburns.

I say, "Hello," and the sky turns dark.

A gale builds and sweeps us into an alley.

We come to in each other's arms.

His hands go for my throat, mine for his.

We are hard. We make guttural noises.

He squeezes my soul up my throat

and out my mouth. It takes flight.

I hear it howl on this day dark like night.

* * *

You pull yourself up slowly

till your eye is at the hole.

You squawk. Your porch

is empty, there is no one

there. In the distance,

you see layers of snow

covering the tent of
Sir Robert Falcon Scott's
doomed expedition. Scott sits
inside with Bowers and Wilson,
while Oates's selfless footprints
fade now, trailing
from the tent
to windswept oblivion.
The tent is tidy, they did
the dishes before they died,
and Scott is clutching his
journal. You can almost
read it from here,
but you gotta really squint:
"It seems a pity, but
I do not think I can
write more ..."
You blink
and it's gone.
The street is dark,
the lights in every home
are off. Cranes reach from the sky
and pluck the roofs
from houses,
silent, silent,
hands begin to appear,
and heads, shoulders,
faces peering over the
tops of walls, men,
women and children crawling

up and out, down
the sides of their homes.
They are free. They crawl
across their lawns and
down the street, past
the 7-Eleven, the laundromat,
past the school and past
the offices.
There is an Arctic waiting,
an Antarctic, a jungle,
a river, there is a great
open field where they can
tilt back their heads
and scream.

Lost Expedition

I fear that
the man who claimed to have cured
his carbuncle by applying
zucchini slices
is no longer leading our
expedition. There were
cries of anguish when it was realized
he had spelunked
one cave too many.
Now we are nine
and we do not play baseball
and we are lost.
We light fires
and fondle our absurd passports.
The monkeys caw in the trees,
they mock us, shower us
with branches
and hunks of bark.
Insects sink their
ugly little pincers
into our necks and ankles.
For courage, we sing
our marching songs,
our climbing songs,
our campfire songs,
our songs of victory,
but without our leader,
our tenor,

we are lost in the wet green noise
of the jungle.
His hair was a silver
that reflected the stars,
his eyes two jet-black
high beams. He had
no carbuncle. He cured
his carbuncle. We
are legion. Our clothes
are soaked through
and caked in mud.
Lodo, they call it here.
Mucho lodo. This is all
we know of their language.
We plod silently
through the muck
for two days
and two hours
and two minutes
and two seconds.
Again we try to sing
and find we've forgotten the words.
We must improvise,
we know this. But
we are followers.
I, for one,
was not chosen as leader.
You can see by my eyes,
my posture, the way my boots
are laced. Look how I cower

when the monkeys scream.
It is pouring rain
for the third day straight,
and we huddle beneath
the densest tree and write.
We write letters.
The rain dissolves our words
as we write, but it
kills time. And it pleases us
to do what the monkeys cannot,
for they cannot write.
Let them jeer their cruel jeers.
We have William Shakespeare.
Another day passes.
Another night.
We sleep with the rain
on our faces, and when we wake
ten minutes later, we pluck
the slugs from our limbs
and the worms from our ears.
We each eat a cracker
and drink each other's tears.
Two more days pass.
We've lost track of the date
and forget the name of our leader,
the foolhardy spelunker.
A week passes.
We are so tired
we laugh uncontrollably.
Armadillos barrel about our feet,

between our legs,
the monkeys blow smoke in our eyes.
They have finished the first chapter
of their book.
The rain has not let up
and we have forgotten what dry is.
We have all changed our names to Lodo
and buried our passports in mud.
We chew on bark.
We decide to rest.
A month creeps by like a thief.
It wears black and leaves no fingerprints.
We play primitive word games
to pass the time.
Our word games are so old
they date back to an era
before language.
Which suits us fine.
We have forgotten how to speak.
We point at the monkeys
who fuck in the trees.
Our eyes are wide with wonder.
Six more hours pass.
Then twelve minutes.
Large drops of rain fall.
They have spaces between them.
We cram ourselves into the spaces
and close our eyes.
We hope that it's all a dream.

Stubborn Furniture

There is a chair in the middle of the room.

A room empty except for a chair.

In the middle of it.

Kick the chair.

Kick it.

Does it have nails?

Like, is it nailed down?

I mean,
did it not fall over
when you kicked it?

Nails is an old trick.

Kick it again.

Clever fucking chair.

Around the Building

From across the road,
I peer at the building.
It is grey, it
rises nine floors.
I work in it. I work
five floors up.
My watch tells me it is 7 a.m.
At 8:30 I will be at my desk,
and I will take the top sheet
from a pile of paper
and I will scrape specks
with a special little knife.
It is my special little knife
and not one defect will go by
unscraped. I am the best in the world
at this. But now
it is 7:02 and I cross the road
and approach the glass doors.
I light a cigarette, like I do
every morning at 7:02,
then I light another, jam
another in my mouth, and
another. I walk to the left,
to the edge of the building,
and I turn the corner. I walk
to the back of the building,
and I turn the corner. I walk
across the back of the building,

around the dumpster, then
turn the corner. I walk
to the front of the building
and turn the corner. Soon I am
at the entrance again. I look at
my watch. It is 7:09. I walk around
the building again. It is 7:17.
A bird smashes into a third-floor
window and falls to my feet.
I place it in my pocket and
circle the building.
It's a different bird
from yesterday. My pocket
is getting full.

I smoke and I walk, and I trace
my hand along the brick. This
building contains me, contains
my thoughts. This building contains
my desk and my phone, my special
little knife, my cubicle. I smoke
and I walk, walk faster, and the traffic
grows. My co-workers begin to arrive,
slipping silently through the door.
I walk around the building. It is
8:26. In four minutes I will be at my desk,
clutching my knife. In four minutes
I will know what to do.

Recreating Jim

Jim falls into an open sewer in downtown Managua. It
is the rainy season. When he emerges, his clothes are
soaked, a page of *La Prensa* is plastered to his leg, his
cigarette is doused, his back is wrecked forever. But he
is still Jim.

Jim dives into a vat of bubbling hatred. His father
emerges legless. His mother is too nice, too nice, and
he hasn't called her for months. Soon his father dies.
Jim soars from the vat, still Jim, swoops low over
Kingston and howls. He wears a cape, which flutters
in the cool air. He is my hero.

Jim drives to Rattlesnake Point and climbs a thirty-foot
rock. He looks down and says, "I've climbed a thirty-foot
rock," smiles for Jo-Anne's camera. He swings from
side to side, and bounces against the rock face, then
comes down, lights up a smoke, still Jim.

I am nine years Jim's junior but my hair is greyer than
his. I've fed his cats and cut his grass and read his
poems. Jim has put his arm around my shoulders. He
has taken from his wallet a picture of his child and
shown it to me. It is his liver. He spins his liver on
his fingertip and talks about it for hours. Jim is sober.
His name is Roque Dalton.

It is inevitable. Jim becomes a great black epileptic dog, gnawing at my hands. He is an animal healing itself, curled up in distant warmth. Jim becomes a most frightening thing. He becomes a man in a race against himself. His fingers can't keep up with his cigarettes. Jim becomes a bus, hurtling north. He pulls a mask down over his face. Jim is a telephone. He abandons his language and learns a new one. Jim recreates Jim.

I can say nothing.

Some Kind of Slowdown in the Intersection

David McFadden lay curled on his side
in an intersection.
David McFadden.
As I stood and watched cars and buses
navigate around his inert figure,
someone appeared beside me and
said, "Who is that lying inert
in the intersection?"
"David McFadden," I told her. "That's
David McFadden lying there on his side
in the intersection. Not often
a Canadian poet stops traffic."
"Well," she replied, "they're not
actually stopping, they're
circumnavigating."
"Well," I argued, "it's an art
still in its infancy."

Looking into My Illness

I was sitting in a sunlit, dusty restaurant
near the railroad tracks that sever
the capital of Guatemala. I had just seen
three quick kids roll a bony old man
in a market I'd been told to avoid
and now I felt like some soup
and a stack of salted tortillas.
These warnings, though:
I'd been warned against everything.
Do not befriend strangers on a train.
Do not fall asleep on the bus.
Do not photograph soldiers.
Do not give money to begging children.
Do not accept the first price given at the market.
Do not eat peeled fruit in the street.
Do not eat meat in the street.
Do not eat in the street.
Avoid political gatherings.
Do not ask locals about the violence.
Do not hike up the volcano alone.
Do not mention the FMLN, the FSLN, or the URNG.
Avoid tap water. Avoid ice.
And now I felt like a bowl of soup
and a stack of salted tortillas.
At a table beside me,
two men slept, snoring loudly.
At a larger table, four men laughed
and pushed at each other,
glanced at me and laughed some more.

A young student shared my table,
carefully printing the alphabet
on a sheet of lined paper.
I dipped a battered spoon
into a chipped bowl of cloudy soup.
I watched as strange grey lumps
rose to the surface and waved at me.
A fly walking the edge of the bowl
watched too.
The soup was warm and rich.
I ate it slowly,
pushing a piece of tortilla into my mouth
after every few sips.
Outside the restaurant,
a pickup truck screeched to a halt.
Two large men grabbed a youth from the road
and heaved him headfirst
into the back of the truck.
A man in uniform stomped on the boy,
then held on tight as the truck raced away.
I looked into the shallow puddle
that covered the bottom of my bowl.
Inside my belly
and through the winding tunnels of my intestines,
an idea was beginning to take shape.
A whole new way of being.
I was to have superdigestion.
I would sweat and ache,
and groan and curse.
I would blast my food from my bowels
almost before I'd eaten it.

Minor Altercation

a poem by Jean Chrétien

I don't know.
What happened?
If you don't know,
the cameras were there.
Some people came in my way,
it might have been ...
I had to go,
so if you are in my way,
I am walking.
So I don't know what happened.
Something happened
to somebody
who should not have been there.

Poem

A half-eaten hamburger.
A broken rubber band.
The inside of my shoe.

Coffee Break

I don't speak English.

It is a bad language.

Give me an onion.

Passed Over

I was passed over
by the streams of broken-down cars
flowing off the edge of the cliff
I was passed over
by the tangled canopies of knotted branches
collapsing on the shoppers in aisle 7
I was passed over
by the 100 eager mothers
waving snapshots of their babies
by the quivering hungry ledger
of a weaving scrum of accountants
by umbrellas concealing hypodermics
and elbows firing hollow-tip bullets
passed over by smiling best-sellers
and growling milkmen
and weeping dentists
and by a horizonful of devious deathclouds
dressed as ticket-takers at a family fun fair
by giant lumbering banana people
drunken ex-models slumped over transistor radios
infant politicians in glittering heels
an expanse of frustrated pavement
a big bug
a very big bug with an armoured thorax
it's got long spindly legs
with hairs poking out
somebody will make a movie about it
it'll lurch through the dirt

and eat other bugs
it will endure heartbreak
and natural disaster
in the end it will triumph
that's some movie
everyone should see it

The Monument

It is Sunday.
It is cold.
The son opens the door
and the father walks in slowly.
Goldberg sits in the back room
reading the sports page,
smoking an invisible cigarette.
Izenberg sits up front,
gazing into the papers
heaped on his tiny desk.
The shop is silent.
Goldberg and Izenberg are silent.
Monuments flank the father
and son — black, grey, white,
single, double, smooth, bevelled —
and the two walk up the aisle
like it's a wedding.
They look from Izenberg to Goldberg,
back to Izenberg, then to Goldberg.
The father places the two under shells,
shuffles them around,
pauses,
shuffles again, then lifts a shell.
It's Izenberg. Izenberg
made the stone for the father's
mother, and now he'll make one
for the father's wife. The father
wants a double, he's thought

long and hard, and he wants
a double. He asks which side
he'll lie on, and imagines the plot,
now covered with snow, and he turns
this way and that, till it finally
makes sense. They wander
among the headstones, father and son,
running their fingers
on the smooth and the rough,
across the letters
in Hebrew and English,
across the flowers, the stars,
the flames. The father remembers
his wife lighting candles
(had they once been devout?),
and he slumps in a chair
and closes his eyes. The son
flips through binders crammed with photos,
the monuments in action, and Izenberg
explains the fine points of each,
while Goldberg, in the back,
is on his third invisible cigarette.
Outside,
the huge willows bend,
a woman drops her keys in the snow,
a little Jewish dog
barks at a lamppost,
and the icebergs
begin to melt.

Happy

I gathered you together and provided you with
comfortable seats so that I may ask you this question:
Did I be happy correctly? Do my smile go on my face
right? In the slots on the backs of the seats in front of
you you should find plenty of paper and some pencils
and I ask you to take your time in answering. Did my
dog like the way I walked him? Am people in general
liking me? Is my niceness genuine in my voice? Am I
enjoying life as you had instructed? Please write your
answers neatly and hand them to my assistant on your
way out the door. And would the last person please tell
the next group I am ready for them.

Billiards and Poison

All the channels say
there'll be a storm.
I'm no Muggins, about
to be stranded for
three days in a pool hall in León
while barrages of rain
pound the metal roof
and Samantha Fox and
Sly Stallone peel
from the yellowed walls, amid
the scrape of chalk against cue,
the din of
anxious laughter,
the yelps of emaciated
dogs, the clack
of the reds, the hiss
of the black.
Our table is the
deformed one in the corner,
chipped and torn, worn
down to its wooden surface.
I play with a warped cue,
and so does Dolores
and equally Joe.
The rain carries typhoid
through the gutters,
to the streets of the poor,
past the tanneries

where men stand knee-deep
in their own young deaths,
past shells of cars
with trees growing through them,
and children play in these streams.
They are famous actors
in Hollywood films
and nothing
frightens them.

After Blackfly Season

The birds are all facing
the wrong direction
like some avian
firing-squad joke

     *

July is the worm
that won't leave the earth
It cries, "Aroint thee!"
and clings to a segmented jesus

     *

The fireflies
compare abdomens
around the
weiner roast

     *

My head is thus —
a beautiful collision

In This World

In this world there were no insects. Or possibly there were *only* insects. Sometimes I have difficulty remembering details. Or perhaps it's a matter of definition. Do we share a vocabulary? Are insects the ones with six legs or the ones with two legs? Are they the ones that walk on the ceiling or the ones that walk on the floor?

And it gets worse. What are those ones that have four legs? It's no piece of cake telling a story. No slice of pie.

Let me start again.

It was a warm, humid night and Bob was unable to sleep. He had too much on his mind and he just couldn't shake that which haunted him. Tired of tossing and turning, he decided to take a walk, or possibly a flight. He got up and walked across the floor, although it may have been the ceiling, and —

I don't think this can really work. I feel somehow that you do not have complete confidence in me as narrator and the crisis may be irreparable. Had I been less moral, or perhaps more clever, I'd simply have chosen one path and stuck to it. There would have been no questions and probably the story would have been finished by now and we could all go get so drunk that we couldn't even stand on our own two legs. Or six legs. Or whatever.

A Message to the Populace

My arms are wide
and welcoming.
Listen:
I found an egg under the hood of a stolen car.
There was writing on it:
POPO THE PIG
SAYS COME TO THE PORK ROAST.
I duly presented it to the authorities,
who rewarded me
with a kiss to the forehead.
I left the station,
something dragging on my shoe.
A piece of paper stuck there.
It said POPO THE PIG
SAYS COME TO THE PORK ROAST.
I ran to the arms of my father,
the hairy loopy arms of my papa.
"POPO THE PIG,"
I said breathlessly.
"What?" he urged, his thumbs
pressing tight against my throat.
"What of it?"
"POPO THE PIG
SAYS COME TO THE PORK ROAST."
My father loosened his grip
and gave me the keys
to the bowling ball.
He said: "The pig

is happy and diversion
vis à vis the barbecue.
Its smile a rainbow from ear to ear.
Now you are a leader.
The community is up in arms.
Present your snout
to the mobs. Establish
mildly a stranglehold
on their grief. We
are history. A slice
from Popo's flank
brings calm and
relentless good posture
to the milling populace."
I accepted the tall man's blessing
and here I am, before you.
Do you know about Popo?
Popo is the happy pig.
Reach deep into your chest
where you have so many hearts.
Give one of those
to each of me.

But, Mister, They No Have Bowling
Balls Before Christ

This supermarket
is my favourite supermarket.

Children plant bombs on the pony ride.
Peacekeepers are blown into the frozen food section.
They begin to think they're niblets.

When the muzak stops,
the shoppers exchange lists.

The shelves are full of disgruntled products.
A box of crackers coughs in my face.
A bottle of soda mocks my beliefs.

I want to buy a bowling ball.
A woman tells me to take a number and wait my turn.

Farmer Gloomy introduces new hybrids.
They make the aisles wiggly.

The rice is so instant it is already eaten.

I replace my tongue with that of a cow.
I am voted fourth most popular shopper.

A rabbi faints in the checkout line.

I leave empty-handed.

The Ring

But in the back of the bar on the
TV that boxer bites off that other
boxer's ear, then his other ear
and his nose. Soon he's eaten the
whole head and is gnawing along
the neck like it was barbecued
corn. "Usually I have my big meal
earlier in the day," he says to
the cameras, "so I can burn it
off before I sleep, but tonight,
I dunno, even with nowhere to
tuck my bib, I just got the craving.
I know I am not the best
role model and I urge the youth
of America to condemn my actions
and do what is right. Never eat
your opponent after lunch or as a
between-meals snack."

The glare of the lights
above the ring, reflecting
off a thousand sweaty
foreheads, refracting through the
curling hissing smoke of a
thousand wagging cigars,
disguises the flight of a moth
that rises from between the
shoulders of the headless boxer
and sails right through the TV

screen, into the bar, where it
alights on the bartender's
shoulder. The bartender does not
yet know his house is empty, his
lover is gone, a terse note
awaits his return,
after a walk through
the cold drizzle, under
flickering streetlamps, through
sidewalks teeming with headless
boxers, their gloved hands raised
in ecstasy.

Landscape

after Larry Fagin

The bright green apple sails over the white fence.
The small running shoe lies in an overgrown field.
The man rappels down the side of a skyscraper.
The happy mice burrow through the rotting garbage.
The Latvian hairdresser leaps with joy.
Malarial flies float dead in the gutter.
A paperboy takes a bow.

One of Those Lakes in Minnesota

We're walking around again
slipping into evening
the insects biting
and we're circling just
one of the lakes in Minnesota
there are hundreds maybe
thousands and Debby's
trying to remember the name
of that sax player who plays
two maybe three instruments at once
and one with his nose and I think
Pharaoh Sanders Lester
Young Art Farmer who I
don't even know if he plays sax
but I used to think his name was
Ant Farmer but no
it's Roland Kirk Debby
remembers it's Roland Kirk she's
listening to these days
trying to learn to play
in spite of her
carpal tunnel syndrome
and speaking of car pools
her van that glorious monster
that brought her and Beth
and Becca and Charlie and
Michael (but not the Michael
who'll come up later in this

poem) to Toronto thru
Lansing Michigan what was it?
two years ago?
well that van
it's dead
just a huge flower-
pot behind her mom's house now
she tells me (that van
was a monster and it
brought these amazing people)
while behind us Michael
the other one
and Judy
are talking
heavy stuff like families
and politics
and Michael's voice is the
black surface of the lake glittering
beneath the stars under
Michael's favourite constellation
which I think is of some animal
a swan or
perhaps bill bissett
and Judy's voice is the smooth
shadows of birds darting
from tree to tree above us
and this lake is endless
tonight I mean we started walking
an hour ago and we're still going
and the insects are eating us

alive and that big lumpy shadow
ahead well it's a raccoon
and Debby's not crazy about
raccoons so we race by while
Michael and Judy stop to
watch and I'm telling you
this is just one of thousands
of lakes in this state but we
could spend a
wonderful life just walking
around this one over and
over again or just once
just one long walk that
takes us around for a life-
time and I say Rahsaan Roland
Kirk to show off I've heard
of him and Debby says yeah
and up by the road a
loud cluster of lights is
passing slowly it's
a motorcycle the
Macarena blaring from it
can you think of anything more
awful? but tonight
it's not awful
it's what makes
the lake
so beautiful
and my birthday passes
then another

then three of Judy's
six of Michael's
five of Debby's and
this is a big lake and a
long night and if
nothing else happens
in our lives
that's just fine
like Roland Kirk
playing perhaps
four instruments at once
one
with his nostrils

The Shopping Mall

At night a shopping mall
is cold and sad.
It flattens itself,
crawls across the
empty expanse of its parking lot,
squeezes under a gleaming archway
that says Shop And Be Happy.
Soon it is
inching along the road;
it has forgotten
its loneliness.
In the glare of the streetlamps,
the mall is indistinguishable
from the pavement.
The telephone wires
don't give it away;
they sway in the crisp air,
mutter amongst themselves.
The fire hydrants are silent,
and so are the mailboxes.
Stray dogs sniff at the creeping mall,
then bound off,
paws ripping lawns,
shrill yaps cracking
the thick clouds above.
Torrents of rain begin to fall
and the mall becomes frightened.
It crawls up to a house

and through an open window.
It is in a small room.
It recognizes the posters on the wall
from its record shop
and the books on the shelf
from its book shop
and the carpet from its
wholesale carpet outlet
and the dresser and desk and bed
from its furniture store
and the lamp on the desk
from its lighting store
and the boy in the bed
from its video arcade.
The shopping mall
creeps up onto the bed
and wraps itself around the boy's chin,
clinging tight to the smooth face.
In the morning, the boy's parents
are astonished when he comes to breakfast.
"You are not yet seven,
but you have a beard,"
says the father, and they
lock him in his room.
Pilgrims come from around the world
to see the bearded boy.
His eyes are wide.
He wants to shave.
He is blessed by the Pope,
and by movie stars,

by hockey players
and famous models.
The steady stream of people
passing by his bed,
night and day,
becomes overwhelming.
The boy is cold and sad.
A policeman looks at a calendar —
the mall went missing
the day the bearded boy appeared!
He hauls the child out of bed
and drags him to the cruiser.
The boy is excited.
He asks the officer to turn on the siren.
He asks the officer to make the red lights flash.
They speed through sleeping streets,
then across an empty parking lot
surrounding a vast, dark chasm.
"I remember this place,"
says the boy,
"I know I've been here before."
The policeman places the child
in the centre of the emptiness
and takes a few steps back.
The boy tugs at his beard,
writhes and wrestles,
thrashes his arms and legs.
The beard is so tight
he can barely breathe.
He lies down exhausted

and falls asleep.
A car pulls into the lot,
and then another.
The officer begins directing traffic.
Soon the boy is teeming with shoppers.
"Where's the cinema?" they ask.
"Where's the Mexican restaurant?"
Shopping at the boy
is not as convenient,
but humans are clever
and patient.
They have weathered many changes.
They are strong.
They adapt.

Carcass Status

Inquiring discreetly about the carcass status
of the hunting jacket upon which fell
my eyes and heart, I was assured
through a cloud of velvet cigarette smoke
that no dead rabbits would turn up
in the lining. I did not wish, like,
to offend the proprietor (of the hunting-jacket joint),
but still I crawled in one red-and-white-checkered
pocket, through the womb of the lining,
and out the other (pocket), finding nothing
but a nuptial carrot, an aubergine —
say that slow: *au-ber-gine* —
and an old token that when examined
under the little microscope I received
on my eleventh birthday
would prove to allow passage
on a mode of transportation
long since extinct.
                              I'm a believer
in caution, my mamá taught me thrift,
but this carcassless jacket, this jacket
impersonating a furry tablecloth
in an Italian restaurant where I once dined
with a Greek professor who could quote,
to the word, the entire catalogue of the Swan

Silvertone Singers, would look good on my
back, keep me warm in these bitter
Canadian winters of yours
where even the dogs shiver
between games of pachisi.

Train to Ottawa in Peacetime

"A bouvier!" she blurted
and shook her neighbour,
who buried his face
deeper in his book.
"Oh, a bouvier —
he's got a bouvier."
She leaned her head to the side
and peered ahead
through the window of the train. And
in his head, his eyes on Thomas Mann,
he wondered: A dry red to go with veal?
Something to hang beside a Monet?
Some high-end touring auto?
What the hell
is a bouvier?
Perhaps a flower.
"But that seems silly," she said,
"to walk your dog by the
railroad track. Young men!"
Young men are scoundrels — he
read her mind, the train
grinding to a halt. Their language,
the way they dress, their
reluctance to give up their seats.
"Why are we stopped?" the woman
spluttered. "My daughter will be
waiting, we haven't seen each —
Oh look, the man from the train,

he's with the bouvier man, he's
walking beside — Can you see? —
He's walking beside the train with —
But where's the dog? Oh, that
beautiful bouvier!" He wrenched
his face from the book. The
train began to move. A dog —
its name, in dog,
was Lieutenant Gabriél
Ernesto López —
dead, lay in the ravine
by the tracks, considering
all it had done, all
it had wanted to do.

Bulletin

We interrupt this poem
for an important bulletin,
for a stunning medical breakthrough,
for a boxing match,
for a glass of 1934 chardonnay,
for the discovery of life on other planets,
for little Jimmy's new leg brace,
for a derailed train, its passengers screaming,
for an appointment with your therapist,
for an empty bird's nest,
for a few tips on nostril depilation,
for an urgent meeting by world leaders,
for a cigarette, the last in the pack,
for a frayed electrical cord,
for a yodelling contest,
for anything,
for god's sake,
but the poem.

After the Event, but Before the Thing
That Happened

I ran from the lightning. I ran from the legless duck.
I ran from the collapsing building. I ran from the bad
boy. I ran from the cob of corn. I ran from the incorrect
professor. I ran from Walking After Midnight. I ran
from the flailing midwife. I ran from the stench. I ran
from the collapsing democracy. I ran from the happy
dreidl. I ran from the moon's gaunt face. I ran from my
sister's shadow. I ran from the porcelain antelope. I ran
from the runaway station wagon. I ran from my sense of
humour. I ran from a lump. I ran from alcohol and
flashlights. I ran from peeling wallpaper. I ran from
bondage. I ran from a Hardy Boys novel and left Chet
Morton behind. I ran from television. I ran from
Immanuel Kant. I ran from off-key troubadors. I ran
from the axe. I ran from adolescence. I ran from the
sneaky cartoon. I ran from cost-effectiveness. I ran from
the limp squeezebox. I ran from chicken bones. I ran
from the fascist clip-art. I ran from the constant
defender. I ran from the shadow of a cloud pursuing me
across a desert whose sands spilled over every horizon.

40 Lines of Explanation

I emerge from the diner splattered by ketchup
fall prey to a falling piano —
well almost — I leap to the side
like a guy leaping sideways
an evasion I do not condone
but just a block away
my feet get tangled in the next day's news
and I tumble ungracefully to the pavement
thrash amid the passing shoes
until finally I grab a random ankle
and I'm dragged 40 kilometres
or maybe it's blocks
perhaps it's 40 years
I'm dragged up 40 steps, or down them
I'm slapped hard across the face 40 times
and 40 gentle kisses rain upon my brow
and I earn $40 and I spend $40
I achieve and I squander
I write a song and lose my voice
and my pockets are inside out
my shoes on backwards
so I always walk in the wrong direction
I paint my glasses black and laugh
and a man stops me in the street
"It is futile," he says
"you can never — "

(There's something about blazing a trail
and leaving one of destruction in my wake
and something else about grinning radiators
a fleeting reference to sporadic weeping
and one to standing on a narrow dirt path
on the side of a hill in northern Guatemala
and to Syd and Shirley, and July 18, 1959
and a fear of asking directions
a lucky habit of getting lost)

I turn a corner and there's another corner
and another corner beyond that corner
they told me to breathe and always remember
and though I forget what I was to remember
I respire, comrade, I respire

The Big Chair

A man causes chaos in his house.
His family flees, finds shelter.
Here there is much light.
Here the clocks function.
Here the children learn to hunt.
Meals are served on plates.
The earth does not shift.
A woman wears a hat of fruit;
she sings into a microphone.
Each morning a calf is born.
Children may select their facial features.
It is safe here.

A man lies on a suspension bridge,
curled in a ball.
He closes his eyes
and doesn't breathe.

Red Beret

Your room awaits you
at the Al Rashid
where your Parisian students
bellydance across the scuffed
and spat-upon mosaic of
George Bush, wanted for crimes
against people and incubators
and truth, and perhaps you
yearn to plant your feet
right here, or maybe there, or
over in that expanse of green,
or that brown
as vast as your eyes.
Plant yourself and soon
a small combo of contradictions
will sprout to accompany you
on a be-bop "Bésame Mucho"
or perhaps "Strange Fruit"
as sung through the smouldering
throat of a violently imploding
Billie Holiday, circa, say, 1957.
But enough of Birdland, we're
talking about agriculture, and you with
one foot planted in fact and
the other scrambling towards fiction,
and you set a tape recorder
by your bedside
and the next morning

you hear your own voice
speaking a language
you don't understand, and you strap
yourself to a chair and
interrogate yourself, depriving
the prisoner of sleep and food and
ballet. But enough about you, let's talk
about *you*, and your
profound and complex beauty
like, say, Billie Holiday, circa 1957.
A cigarette — it is not mine
and it is not yours — burns on the
edge of a coffee table notched
with family secrets, and through
the haze a camera flashes.
You are still.
A shadow blacker than your hair
splatters against
an orange horizon
and in the distance
buildings collapse,
sirens wail.
Debris sails gently to the
ground around us
like autumn leaves.
You stand in an elevator,
wrapped in a bathrobe.
The door slides open
and words tumble in,
some of them your own. I

am always looking for silence,
but when I tear open my chest
I am filled with the crash
of machinery, some terrible din.
You race through the streets,
clutching your red beret, while
cities flash by like cartoons:
Baghdad, Jerusalem, Vancouver,
Paris, Beirut.

In the distance,
a kilometre from the shore,
a fisherman rubs his rough jaw,
raises his eyes to the sun,
resumes his life as a dot,
a fleck, a sparkle
on the face of the globe.

The Cow

My line went taut,
I woke from an allergic slumber,
knew I'd caught a cow
(my father long ago had taught me how).
I reeled its living carcass in
and sat it down beside me on the rock.
We'd have a talk. But when I looked
into its mucoid eyes, and it
into mine, all red from last night's
smoke and self-loathing and wine,
I knew I'd throw it back.

As it crossed its legs, adjusted its cross,
and gazed across the water, I plunged a hand
into the gash my hook had ripped in its chest.
I felt its heart, its lungs, its ribs, its steak.
I felt its warm blood bathe my fingers clean.
I saw my future, black and white,
a desert, where, among the cacti,
human skulls and bovine skulls from John Ford films
lulled and roosted and mised their scènes together.

My daddy wore an apron — "I'm the Chef" —
my mama fussed about a picnic table.
Their own parents huddled fetid in
the bowels of a boat, traversing a
desert of water (their brothers and sisters
marching to slaughter) to give birth to
my daddy and his apron and my mama.

When I withdrew my hand from the bowels
of my prize-winning catch, I heard flies
flying hungrily, buzzing the blood,
and I knew we were brothers,
or brother and sister,
and I was a moo-cow and it was
a killer. I bowed my head, tenderized,
and the cow threw me back in.

Home Shopping

In this city, where I was once in love, transcendentally
so, deliriously so, such that my friends were concerned
about me; in this city, not my own, where every bar and
café is a landmark, every park bench, every broken tree
branch, every pocket of air we once passed through; in
this city, where once our lips met so tentatively, where
we gazed endlessly and stupidly into one another's eyes,
where we embraced with a rapturous fear and
desperation; in this city, in this tiny room, in this dark
night, in this late late hour, my face absorbs the glow of
the television, the flickering dance of images, and I
watch the numbers flash upon the screen, the numbers
and instructions and conditions, and I command my
arm to command my hand to command my fingers —
it's such a tedious hierarchy, the channels you must go
through for such a simple act — to dial those numbers,
and my fingers obey, stumbling tiredly on the plastic
numbers of the telephone, a telephone that sends
signals through cables that once carried yearning
declarations of love, and murmurs uttered through quiet
tears of relief and bliss; and I say into the phone, I open
my mouth and say, here, in the dark isolation of the
middle of the night, in this once-magical city: "Yes, I
would like the salad spinner, the Salad Spinner 2000."
I say, "Please send me the Deluxe Toilet Splatter Shield,
I just saw it on TV." I say, "I want the four-CD set
of *Best-Loved Songs of Terminal Illness* and the
accompanying collection of *Posthumously Penned*

Melodies of Mantovani." I practically bark into the phone,
"I want it now — the Arnold Palmer Hair Restoration
Kit — I can barely wait!" I murmur in a voice firm but
passionate, "I am lying on my sofa and it came to me
through my television, like an angel of mercy, the Super
Egg Squarer, I want to make my eggs square, send it
immediately, and include the bonus combination Rice
Fluffer and Ceiling De-Cobwebber, but only if I order
now, right this minute, this offer will not be repeated,
operators are standing by." And I put down the phone,
through an intricate series of neural commands,
the physiological details of which can be acquired
elsewhere, it's beyond the scope of my concern and
responsibility, and I pull my knees to my chest and close
my eyes, and the sounds of the television wash over my
ears and I can feel its luminescence paint my face, and I
wait, and I sleep and wait, wait four to six weeks, in this
tiny room in this city where once I knew with a visceral
certainty the meaning of love, the exquisite, irreversible
flutterings of the heart, and outside, beyond these
walls, people fall and get up, buses screech to a halt,
governments collapse, dogs are neutered, dead leaves
are whipped up by the cold wind, a child blows out her
birthday candles, and eventually, inevitably, my doorbell
rings, or there is a knock at the door, the exact nature of
the technology is beyond the range of my knowledge,
and men in caps and uniforms march in and construct
a tower of boxes, gradually, over days and weeks and
months, more and more boxes accumulate, and I lie on
my side on the sofa in front of the television, and I

know that I am on the right track, that I am healing,
that salvation lies in my ever-accumulating acquisitions,
delivered to me from warehouses across the continent.
I am in a city where I had known a love that had
transformed my very biology, rearranged the synapses of
my brain, reshaped and renamed every organ in my gut,
made me dizzy and made me skinny. But now I am in
control, and from the sofa headquarters of my inert
body, my atrophying limbs, my glowing angel's visage,
I make things come to me, box after box after box,
hefted by identical men in identical caps and uniforms,
and each box is some essential nutrient, sap for my
branches, oil for my generator, and I feel myself heal,
gradually heal, and, lest I be dislodged, I clutch the
edges of this sofa in this tiny room slapped onto one
molecule of this huge wobbling sphere hurtling
relentlessly through an endless expanse of black, lit
only by stars.

The Shape of Things to Come

A translucent gizmo
bobs against
the ceiling.

My round head
bobs against
the pillow.

A happy fish
bobs against
the rocks.

Bring on
another of those
century things
for which
you're so famous
for.

January 1, 2000

The Rec Room

We drag our faces gently along
the plywood-panelled walls, our
hair skimming the particle-board
ceiling. This is where our dreams lie,
down here, in the forgotten
room of the house where we've lived
so long. We excavate artifacts:
a fishing trophy, a collapsed
clay ashtray, the awe-inspiring
Strange Change Toy (from
Mattel), a mitten sporting an
embroidered moose, a social
studies project from Grade 4
(every word copied
from the 1966 *World Book*
Encyclopedia), a little plastic
Indian, a Leo Sayer album
from before he went disco
(though we have no problem
with disco), a photo of Mother
and Father at the Top Hat Club,
circa 1948, a bowling shoe
that looks brand-new, a flower
pressed between the pages
of *Cheaper by the Dozen*,
a shot glass, a baseball stamped
with Sandy Koufax's signature,
and finally

my heart, we almost didn't notice it,
pulsating gently in the corner,
waiting for someone to
ask it to dance. The balloons
come loose from the ceiling
and drift to the floor. Up the stairs
and outside, out on the street,
station wagons glide silently by,
and a boy runs across the lawn,
chasing a yarmulke
snagged by the wind.

Hospitality

Breakfast in my
hotel room. Autumn.
In my fruit salad,
the biggest orange seed
I've ever seen.
The room becomes dark.
I look to the window.
The curtains are drawn.
Hold on a sec — does
drawn mean open or closed?
Or perhaps
scrawled on the wall.
I fumble for the phone.
The woman at the desk answers.
I say to her, "Look,
my curtain is drawn.
My room is dark.
The orange pit is
overwhelming. Can you please
send someone up
to draw a window?
Someone with a steady hand —
an intern will do."

When I come to, I am tucked
into bed. On the table beside me
sits a glass of water, some
loose change, Graham Greene's

The Comedians, open to page 77:
"the pleated screen
in the unnecessary fireplace."
On the bedsheet
is an enormous pit. I go
to brush it away,
but I have no arms

or perhaps too many to choose from.
A nurse enters. A scream
from the hallway. Winter morning.
A cool hand across my brow.
My eyes are stuck shut —
a new adhesive
developed just for me.
A thermometer rattles against
my teeth. I am against
capitalism. Soft lips
against my cheek. Okay,
I've made my point.
I'll tell you exactly
what I remember:

I was sitting on a bench
outside the mall. I was
eating a taco. The taco
contained lettuce, tomatoes,
ground beef, orange cheese,
refried beans, Tabasco sauce.
A woman ran past me.

She said,
"A man is in the bank
with a gun. A man's head
fell off when he tried
to stop him. A teller lies
on the floor and a phone
is off the hook."
I followed her to her car,
trying to eat my taco.
I said, "I keep confusing this moment
with when John Kennedy
died. No, wait, that's
later, that's what'll happen
much later in my life, because
John Kennedy is still alive.
No, wait, what year is it?"
Her car sped off. She stayed behind,
reached for my hand.
I'm just kidding — she
was in the car. I waved
with what was left of my taco.

Monkeys

We were talking about monkeys and monkey cinema.
Planet of the Apes, of course — that goes without
saying. All the parts: Beneath, Battle For, Escape From,
they were all good. Monkey Business, someone said,
and someone said that was the Marx Brothers, and
someone else said, yeah, but there was also one with
Cary Grant and Marilyn Monroe. And Ed, how about Ed,
that monkey baseball player, he sure could pitch, and all
those Clint Eastwood orangutans. They were big and
orange. We wondered about why there were no
proboscis monkey films — those'd for sure be solid hits
if the monkey was paired up with, for example, Harvey
Keitel or maybe Reese Witherspoon. A scientist
proboscis monkey would work, or even a surfer
proboscis monkey. Or a proboscis monkey in a
classroom that everyone thought was just a new student
and it aced all the tests. Someone mentioned Gorillas in
the Mist, and we wondered if it was a monkey movie,
because, in fact, none of the monkeys wore clothes in
that one. You have to wear clothes to be a monkey
movie. Otherwise what's the point? Then someone said
something about bananas and it reminded us about
food and the guy whose house we were at offered us
grilled cheese sandwiches and someone said how when
they were a kid they thought it was "girl cheese
sandwiches" and then we were off talking about
sandwiches. In those days, we thought we'd live forever.
Nothing could stop us.

Sueño Perdido

after Valery Larbaud

Oh endless grey clouds choking the sky,
black moon, invisible stars,
distant squeal of tires beneath
the shell of a car with a tree growing through it;
oh various trembling monsters
that lurch through cold empty cellars,
and whose scribbled claws swipe from beneath my bed,
who await me in places I'll never go; oh
constant clatter of locomotives through
my chest, tiny trembling pigeon
lodged in my bowels, ill-formed kernels of love
glittering in the back of my throat,
in my shoulders, in the palms of my hands;
oh vivid memories of decades before my birth,
of all the pain I've caused, and the pain for which
I bear no blame, the peaceful dreams
of those dear to me, the misspellings on
eroded headstones shrouded in mist; oh chaos,
exhaustion, bliss, confusion, serenity, blankness,
panic, quiet, quiet;
oh endless roaring clouds
rolling over my head, I offer you this:
my lost sleep.

Razovsky at Peace

On the street, a guy says to Razovsky,
"Over there, behind those buildings:
nature." Razovsky goes.
In nature, it is much quieter.
There is no TV, but there's animals,
which are like TV but furrier.
In nature, Razovsky is damp.
His arms and legs itch. He is
covered in insects.
Razovsky talks, shouts:
in nature, he can't understand
his own words. They disappear
into trees, behind rocks, become
dew. Razovsky's shoes slide
along the slick leaves that carpet
this enormous living room.
A squirrel comes round a tree trunk,
its head stretched out, its nostrils
twitching. Razovsky twitches back.
They stare, time passes,
they stare. The squirrel's watery eyes
blink. Razovsky obeys.
He lies down in the moist leaves,
lets his limbs go limp.
Beyond the highest branches of the trees,
through the spaces the leaves leave,
he sees the sky, the clouds. He is
engulfed by screeches and scratchings

and thuds and buzzings. The songs
of birds he cannot name. He was never
good at this stuff.

He closes his eyes, lets the sky
suck itself back into the sky.
Everything is orderly. For example:
a potato-chip bag bounces near in a breeze.
It becomes wedged between two rocks,
flutters, rustles.
Time passes. Razovsky becomes
part of the ground. The chip bag
becomes a butterfly, as ordained
by nature; it struggles from its
cocoon, bats its wings,
tugs frantically,
but still it is lodged
between the rocks. Razovsky
is not surprised.
He looks up from the ground
at the same moment
he looks down from the trees.
His eyes meet his eyes.
There is a flicker
of recognition.

Poodles on Pedestals

I turned right instead of left
as I left
Papa Madonna Doughnut
Paradise, a green parakeet
nipping at my heels,
pecking, peckish.
It is because I
did not know my
right from left,
never have, my
up from down neither,
always been useless
at this, like at
everything else, that I
wound up
automisnavigating,
panicking,
stumbling through
an unmarked door
off an unmarked alley
that smelled like rotting
cartographers. And there
did I behold a sight
more, um, poodley, than
I had ever beheld: a hallway
stretched forever before me,
and up one side and
down the other, or down

that side and up this one,
poodles of every size
and shape, perched on
marble pedestals. These were
not those poodles you see
at pie-eating contests
or thumbing rides on
desert highways; these
were that other kind,
the poodles our parents
warned us about: sniffing,
lascivious, quivering,
commanding. I read the little
nameplate on each pedestal:
Conrad, Verity, Lozenge,
Cordera, Prince Happy Happy,
Felix, Faulkner, Pinky,
Sportspage, Parquet Ralphy
of Russell Hill Road, Schlepp,
Pol Pot, Montgomery Clift,
Norman, Veronica,
and another Norman.
They said something to me
about rhyming couplets
that didn't rhyme, about
my grandpa and when Rufus
got run over, about
the end of capitalism,
when everything would be
lower-case, about

that I should be
more careful how human I try
to be. I nodded and shook
every one of their paws — did
I already tell you this? — I shook
all their paws, by which I mean
one each, one paw on each
dog, not all four.
So later, after brunch —
I mean, a bunch
of other stuff,
on my way home,
a boy on the bus
wore a black bow tie
and a pale green
name tag: Elder Twitchell.
Imagine a tornado
sucks him out the window
and into the sky. Imagine
him dead. Imagine a panel
of celestial poodles
decides his fate. The fear
that once consumed me,
that clutched my guts
as I tried to sleep,
was sucked out the window
in his place.

We Got Punched

Mark Laba and I were walking along Spadina Avenue.
It was 1977. We were still in high school.
Mark pretended to kick in a shop window
and then there was a guy walking up between us.

(Mark and I had been friends since 1962 or 1963,
when we were just a few years old. We had played
together, we drew together, we ran an insect cemetery.
Business was slow, so we killed bugs ourselves
and buried them in Wrigley's Spearmint Gum wrappers.)

We were on our way to the Horseshoe Tavern to see Robbie Rox.
This guy stopped in front of us and yelled something
I can no longer remember, not necessarily because
it happened 24 years ago, but because I have a bad memory.

(Mark and I played in Wilmington Park, just south
of Bathurst Manor Plaza where we bought our gum
and our *Mad* magazines. Once we were on the monkey bars
and another kid tried to move in on them, and I said
that my dad owned the playground, and I said,
"I swear to the Jewish Torah." Later, I felt guilty for lying.)

The guy stopped and we kept walking and as we walked by
he punched us in the face, both fists at once, like twin
torpedoes. He yelled, "That what you want?" or something like that,
and across the road some guys were laughing, and it was a hot
summer day, and me or Mark said to Mark or me, "Run!"

(Mark and I both had only brothers, older brothers. My brother
                                                    Barry
was friends with his brother Marty, so that's how we met.
We phoned each other when my number was 633-4365 — we
                                                    called it
Melrose 3-4365 then — and his was 633-4822, and he asked for
"Ross" and I asked for "Laba." And now we've each had
a brother die, but not Barry or Marty — Owen and Michael.)

We ran down Spadina and ducked into a deli, because
there were delis on Spadina then, and we ran downstairs
to the washroom and looked at ourselves. My T-shirt was splashed
with blood that gushed from my mouth. Mark had lost his glasses
and his eyebrow was bruised. We were chilled. We shook.

(A dozen years later we had a falling-out, and soon he moved
to Vancouver and I stayed in Toronto, and a few more years passed
till we talked, and now we're friends, though we don't
talk much, we don't talk much, we don't talk much.)

We skipped Robbie Rox and we went to the apartment of
my friends Mike and Jeannie, who were older than us, and Mike
wasn't home, but Jeannie gave us vodka, which because of our age
was probably illegal so I will not mention her last name here, okay,
and soon we calmed down and the pain subsided.

(I wrote a really bad poem about this in 1978, called "Witness to
the Execution," and for this I ask your forgiveness. And for this
                                                    poem,
too, I ask your forgiveness. I am old now, and feeble, and have lost
my powers of imagination.)

Meaningless Encounters with Random Citizens

We call this here a "doughnut shop,"
do you understand what I'm saying,
where we sit and smoke, drink coffee,
read paperback novels
we found on the sidewalk.
It is here we twiddle our brain circuitry,
try to become machines,
machines are way better,
and better still if they could cry.
And people sit down beside us,
people we do not know,
and Thelma pounds the cash
with the side of her fist,
and we — we stare blankly
and we fall in love
and kill and ask
for a quarter, bum
filterless cigarettes and we
talk about that movie we saw
with Alain Delon, remember
his blond beauty,
and we recall our ancestry,
piece together bits of photos
we find in our wallets.
We've been here
since we woke up,
some of us were
born here, christened Cruller,

a couple are dead
in the booth in the corner.
Thelma delivers the last rites,
pours some more coffees. Her
brother was lost
on the side of a mountain.
Crowd control is sexy,
see what I mean,
we twist and come
in the blast
of the water cannon,
here where my grandpa
always ordered
a raised chocolate; my pappy
ordered a Hawaiian sprinkle;
and I, a Modern Young Man
with a television for a head
and an extra digit on each hand,
order a powdery
plexiglas golem,
I could eat a whole box.
A thousand leaves drift
from the ceiling
when Thelma pulls the lever,
and we close our eyes
as if we are one,
and we feel ourselves
evolve.

After the Shiva

Well, there wasn't much room,
so they had me sleep in the bathtub.
There wasn't much room, right?
I practically lived in the bathtub —
I read there, I ate, I slept there.

I pulled the curtains closed
and listened to people piss beside me.

This was my world:
cold enamel against my back;
voices from the other rooms;
a click, then some light;
a click, then some dark.

"Mama," I murmured.
"Mama, bring me a bird.
Papa,
bring me a sky."

Me and the Five Blind Boys of Mississippi Go to Mars

Kindergarten. A mat.
Raisins and milk.
Todd hits me on the hand.
The rope ladder. Summer.
Her swimming pool. Toes.
A sewing machine.
Cow's tongue on
the cutting board.
Grandpa in pyjamas.
Miss Acker. Mrs
Myers. Miss
Leibovitz.
The driveway.
Marky. Stevie. Saturday wrestling.
The Flying Kangaroos.
The Fabulous Love Brothers
(Reginald and Hartford).
Later, even after now, me and the
Five Blind Boys of Mississippi
go to Mars.

Invitation to Love

Hi there, my name is Stuart.
I'm 41. I have brown hair —
at least I used to have brown hair,
it's grey now. I have brown eyes —
well, I used to have brown eyes,
but I poked them out.
I'm 5 foot 9 when I'm standing straight,
though normally I'm hunched over.
I don't really believe in astrology,
but I'm a Cancer, which seems appropriate,
and I was born in 1959, the Year of the Pig,
although I did do a couple of dishes last week
before I got distracted. Things I enjoy ...
I enjoy moping about the state of the world
and worrying about missile attacks
by rogue states,
and I enjoy just spending an evening by the fireplace,
thinking about leaping into it.
I also like to drink alone
and watch Meat Loaf and Pat Benatar videos.
I consider myself a nature person,
and have a dead plant on my window sill,
but I'm not sure what kind it is.
I am employed, and I love my job
but I fear I may soon get fired
because they're always downsizing.
I'm looking for that special someone
who will say nice things to me

because my self-esteem's real low
(it's off the scale in this psychology test I took
that's named after two German psychiatrists),
and basically I'm looking for someone
I might be able to drag down with me.
If you're interested,
maybe we can work something out.

The Catch

The last time I saw her I was hauling records from the apartment on Maitland we had shared for years. She couldn't believe how few I was leaving her, but hell, I'd bought them all. We were both so relieved.

The last time I saw her was in the *plaza* in Antigua, Guatemala. I thought we were done with tears weeks earlier, but there they were again, in my eyes, and perhaps in hers. She told me to look after myself and to go to Mexico.

The last time I saw her was at the Maastricht train station, from which I would travel to Schiphol for a 4 a.m. flight. Tears covered my face and she kissed me goodbye, apologizing for bringing me so far from home.

The last time I saw her was in her car, in front of my apartment on Dundonald, after an absurd trip to the Group of Seven collection in Kleinburg. Tears filled her wide eyes. I apologized for pulling the rug out from under her.

The last time I saw her was in the narrow lane beside the home we had shared on Palmerston. I had arrived to meet my movers. She and I hugged. Tears on her face. I told her to take care.

The last time I saw her it was 4 in the morning and we stood at Bloor and Christie. My face: tears and snot. Her eyes: pity and concern. She told me to get some sleep, to look after myself.

The last time I saw her was in her apartment on Huron. I was tired. There was a hug, a kiss. No tears. When I walked out the door, she congratulated me. For the first time, I had turned the right way down the corridor.

Razovsky at Night

In a distant corner of Razovsky's bedroom
— beyond the crates, the dying plants,
the empty dresser, the hat rack,
beyond a stack of unanswered letters,
a broken lamp, the photos of relatives
whose names he doesn't know —
cowers his bed, a thing so short and narrow
he has to fold in his legs
and suck in his guts to fit on it.
Above the bed hangs a painting
of a rabbi, his hands
clutching oars as he struggles
to steer his small boat
through a dark wall of foaming waves
bearing down on him
like a startled bear.
Through the open window,
a cool breeze swirls in, kicking up
loose papers like they are dry leaves.
It is here, each night, in this comfort
and serenity, that Razovsky lays down
his tired body and chomps for the worm
that writhes on the bobbing hook of sleep.

Here are his dreams:
He dreams he is being pursued.
He dreams he is being pursued.
He dreams he is being pursued.

He dreams he is a small child
and he's climbed a set of monkey bars
so high he cannot get down.
He dreams he is in hospital.
He dreams he is fishing
with his cousins, and suddenly
they're gone, and he is alone
on the water. He dreams
he has been caught.

Every hour or so, Razovsky wakes,
and his brain swims for a memory:
a set of lips soft and warm
on his forehead; a car
backfiring three blocks away;
he's standing in a windless
and silent field.

And then he's heaved roughly
back into sleep.

Razovsky on Foot

Razovsky bounds through the streets,
his arms outstretched,
his tongue thrust out.
He's trying to capture
a single snowflake.
He runs through traffic,
up onto the sidewalk,
into a park and over the monkey bars,
he runs through the schoolyard,
past his own unborn children
(when will they ever get born?).
Razovsky feels the weight of his feet
as he pushes them into the strip mall,
through the front doors
of the Bathurst Manor deli;
he weaves between tables,
greets the lunch crowd,
and darts out the back door,
his tongue still flapping.
Razovsky runs through Radom
(a town in Poland),
through Minsk (in Russia),
through circuses and cemeteries,
past a streetcar stop
where among the crowd
is the woman he'll marry,
though he doesn't yet know her.
She chases him two blocks

till she grabs his coat
and spins him around.
"What are you doing," she asks,
"running through the street
with your tongue sticking out?
Everyone is talking, you're
the talk of the town!"
Razovsky pulls in his tongue
to answer: "I am simply trying
to catch a snowflake."
The woman grabs his shoulders:
"But there is no snow,
it is summer."
Razovsky feels her warm hands
on him, peers into her dark eyes,
considers the slope of her nose,
and for a moment he thinks
of abandoning his quest.
Then he looks into the clouds:
"All I have done for you —
the candles, the prayers,
the meals, the anger —
can't you start your machine,
that ugly grinding and squealing,
and make for me one stinking snowflake,
one fucking little construction
of intricate ice?" And he thrusts out
his tongue again, stretches a palm
to the sky, and he runs.
Some years later,

tired, unshaven,

he has stopped for a coffee,

hunched over the counter.

Around him men argue

about Dave Keon and Bobby Orr,

spoons clatter to the floor,

the smoke from cigarettes

roars through the air,

and there,

on his knuckle,

Razovsky feels a familiar wetness.

"I remember you," he says.

"I've been looking for you."

Razovsky Rides a Cloud

Razovsky knows he must
finally be sleeping, because
he is cushioned on a cloud
sailing past a jet bound
for Florida, and this is not
possible, this thing
of floating on a cloud.
He must be so light,
and he feels light
inside. He feels his eyes
are lights, their beams
guiding his way. Straight up
the aisle, from the very back,
where the bent old men pray,
the regulars, their *tallitim* hanging
like ancient draperies,
up the aisle
towards the rabbi, the cantor,
the trembling bar-mitzvah boy.
Razovsky marvels at this shul
in the sky, and the
storm of candies
that rains over him. Razovsky
sails over the altar
and through the stained glass,
a little baby
floating in a basket
looking for parents, for

a future, for love.
Jeepers creepers, he's
got racing stripes, he's
wearing pyjamas of cloud,
his glorious sleep
will not end.

AFTERWORD

I was a kid who read Ogden Nash and Rudyard Kipling on top of my Dr. Seuss and Petunia the Duck. Then E.E. Cummings and Edgar Allan Poe and Stephen Crane, who self-published his weird shit. My oldest brother, Barry, showed me John Donne's "The Flea" and I read it a million times. When I was 11, I sent out some poems — hand-printed, on lined paper — for publication in a Toronto daily's weekend magazine. They were rejected, gently. Books By Kids, which later became Annick Press, published me in 1975, when I was 16. It was a lovely book called *The Thing in Exile*, with poems by me and my friends Mark Laba (with whom I'd once run an unsuccessful insect cemetery) and Steve Feldman. Here's one of my poems, untitled, from that strange little anthology:

> sitting on the curb
> the man with no chin
> half-mumbled
> about
> the lack
> of lower
> jaw
> the passers-by laughed at this freak
> but he could not complain
> for if he did
> he'd slice his throat

I'd started doing readings when I was 14 or 15, and *The Thing in Exile* launched a tour of local high schools, where I always figured I was going to get beat up. There'd be mutterings from the class equating "poet" with "faggot." I was the kind of kid who got beat up. Here's one more untitled poem from that old collection:

> the children in
> the Catholic school
> playground
> were being tended

by penguins
dressed as nuns

in the Arctic
the polar bears
were being observed
by nuns
dressed as penguins

it was
an exchange program

The penguin was a recurring motif in my early poems — my trade-mark, in fact. It would later be replaced by hamburgers, and then by poodles, as my work matured.

I soon found myself at AISP, a "free school" in North York. That school, which I still visit, saved my life. Saved me from getting beat up, too, I'll bet. Through AISP, I met a series of guest creative writing instructors — Sam Johnson, David Young, Victor Coleman, Chris Dewdney, Joe Rosenblatt. Rosenblatt said there was nothing worth salvaging in any of the 30 poems I showed him, except one, "Ritual of the Concrete Penguins." I got introduced to a lot of freaky writing. Around that time, I also attended workshops downtown with the poet George Miller and did some grunt work for poet/anthologist John Robert Colombo, who critiqued my poems in exchange.

With Mark Laba, I went to readings by Rosenblatt, bill bissett, the Four Horsemen. Mark and I began writing and performing our own sound poems, things like "Jacques Cousteau and the Amazing Sea Monkeys" and "Fate Drives a Gold Mustang." They went over pretty well and we did it for a decade, screaming and chanting and mumbling in front of an audience. (Much later, I screamed, chanted, and mumbled in collaboration with poet and composer Gary Barwin, and I briefly fronted a band called the Angry Shoppers when their singer quit.) Giving readings became my favourite part of being a writer.

Meanwhile, in 1978, I published my first chapbook, *He Counted His Fingers, He Counted His Toes*, under the imprint Proper Tales Press (I liked how *normal* that sounded). It included a dreadful poem for the recently deceased punk Sid Vicious called "Vicious Obituary." I made 50 copies of this 12-pager on my dad's office photocopier and sold 13 of them for 50 cents a pop at a reading I gave at the Axeltree Coffeehouse. This bought me an excellent Chinese dinner, much better than the 85-cent lunch combo Laba and I used to skip classes for at Kwong Chow. The next year, inspired by literary street vendors Don Garner and Crad Kilodney, I printed up 1,000 copies of a new poetry and fiction chapbook and began selling my stuff on Yonge Street. Did that for over a decade, distributing about 7,000 books and chapbooks for $2 to $5. I made a lot of friends on the street and met a lot of strange people. I ducked the occasional fist from a drunk and wiped off the occasional gob of spit from someone respectable who thought I should "get a job."

I was reading poetry like crazy, too: Americans James Tate, Ron Padgett, and Mark Strand, Canadians Joe Rosenblatt and David McFadden, the Austrian George Trakl, the Chilean Nicanor Parra, a bunch of surrealists. On Sundays I played chess over at Crad's, the football game silent on the TV. He showed me his crank letters, his vanity-press collection, and once a woman with three breasts in a porn mag he wrote for. And at York University, I studied film theory under Robin Wood, who would become a good friend. Robin said *The Texas Chain Saw Massacre* was among the most distinguished American films of the 1970s, and that excited the hell out of me. Films sparked my writing nearly as much as books.

In the course of an interview for York's student newspaper, I met poet, playwright, and novelist Tom Walmsley, who had just won Pulp Press's 3-Day Novel contest with his punk classic *Doctor Tin*. His writing was raw and visceral, and when I asked him about a savage review his current play had received, he said he'd like to piss in the critic's mouth. He scared the hell out of me. We became friends. I met the brilliant Opal Louis Nations, an absurdist writer and the editor of Strange Faeces Press, after I reviewed one of his books. These two guys — different in every conceivable way — both fed my hunger for underground literature.

In the street, with a sign around my neck that read "Writer Going to Hell: Buy My Books," I met poet jwcurry, the publisher of Curvd H&z and *Industrial Sabotage*. His obsessive publication in ephemeral forms, and his formal adventurousness, fuelled me. We talked into the early mornings in his cluttered Toronto apartment. This was it — this was the world: small press literature. In 1982 I started up *Mondo Hunkamooga: A Journal of Small Press Reviews*, the first of several litmags with dumb names that I would produce. In 1985, along with Nick Power, who was publishing under his imprint Gesture Press, I ran Meet the Presses, a monthly mini-small-press-fair that lasted a year. In '87, Nick and I founded the Toronto Small Press Book Fair, an event that still goes, a dozen coordinators later.

All this — the publishing, the readings and the reading, the selling, the mags — became inseparable from my writing practise. I wrote stuff, I cranked out copies. I wrote some more, cranked out some more. In 1989 I published a chapbook of hero-worship poems called *Ladies & Gentlemen, Mr. Ron Padgett*. I sent Padgett a copy and received a postcard in return: "Dear Stuart Ross, Best book I ever read. Sincerely, Ron Padgett." Later that year, my favourite Canadian poet, Jim Smith, dragged me off for the first of my three trips to Central America. With a few other Canadians, we put together a Canada booth at the Sandinistas' International Book Fair in Managua, Nicaragua (the Canadian government had chosen not to send a delegation). I'd never seen anything like that ruined city. It was bleak and absurd, like a Samuel Beckett novel.

In the 1990s, I began issuing single-poem leaflets for readings I gave, so people would have something concrete to take home with them. I was also publishing the works of others — usually things I wished I'd written myself. Chapbooks by Kevin Connolly, Lillian Necakov, Opal Nations, Gil Adamson, Joe Brainard, Alice Burdick, and Richard Huttel. Lots of others, too. My own chapbooks and ephemera had been coming out since the 1980s from Connolly's Pink Dog Press, curry's Curvd H&z, Smith's The Front, David UU's Silver Birch Press, and Clint Burnham and Katy Chan's Contra Mundo. As my "real" books started emerging in the mid-'90s (poetry from ECW and fiction from Bev Daurio's Mercury Press), I continued making my own books and leaflets and broadsides.

My mom, born Shirley Blatt, who had held the microphone while I read "The Charge of the Light Brigade" into a reel-to-reel tape recorder at age six, died in 1995. Jewish stuff started creeping into my writing. Death does that. My brother Owen died in 2000, and my dad, Sydney, died in 2001. I've rarely been able to write about my mother, but my father generated poems in me years before his death. His family name was Razovsky, a name I wish we'd kept, and before he died I told him my next book'd be called *Razovsky at Peace*, after a poem I'd written the year before. He never got my poems, but he thought that was pretty funny.

*

This book is divided into two sections. "Poems New" gathers work written since the publication of *Razovsky at Peace* in 2001. "Poems Selected" consists of poems written between 1978 and 2001, in near-chronological order. Many of those poems were published in my three books from ECW Press, and others previously appeared in chapbooks, leaflets, and postcards from various very small presses, including my own. Some of the poems, like "Frank Poem #1," written during my surreal stint as a copyeditor at Harlequin Books in the early 1990s, have never been published before.

It was tough to pinpoint the year I wrote many of these poems. For about half, I had dated manuscripts; others held clues to their conception date (I began writing about Central America only after my first trip there in 1989, for example, though "17 Poses: For Beginners and Advanced," from 1984, has a poet dropped from an airplane); others I've ordered through pure guesswork. I began "Sitting by the Judas Hole" around 1993, but didn't complete it until 1998 for a chapbook, then tweaked it in 1999 for *Farmer Gloomy's New Hybrid*. I've ordered it by its birthdate here, because that's when I wrote the bulk of it. Besides, it's probably a poem I wouldn't have conceived in 1998.

I've tried to choose poems that represent my poetry over the past quarter-century and that might still amuse or bug a reader. Resisting the temptation to edit wholesale, I've tinkered with the occasional punctuation mark or line break, made a judicious excision here and there. Christ, I need a shave!

Stuart Ross
Toronto, March 2003

ACKNOWLEDGEMENTS

Some of the poems here have been previously published, occasionally in slightly different form, in the magazines *Akropolis, B After C, Blue Moon, Bomb Threat Checklist, CB: a poetry magazine, Eat Me Literally, Geist, Harper's, HIJ, In Tents, Industrial Sabotage, Lost & Found Times, Oveja Negra, Oversion, Perpetual Motion Machine, Queen Street Quarterly, Saturday Night, Taddle Creek, Thalia-Bullwinkle Review, This Magazine, WHAT!*; in the anthologies *all of my poems are about you* (1993), *Big Eyed Love Child of the Instant Anthology* (Toronto Small Press Fair, 1999), *Blurred Blue Tattoo of the Instant Anthology* (Toronto Small Press Fair, 2002), *Bride of the Instant Anthology* (Toronto Small Press Fair, 1998), *Carnival: A Scream in High Park Reader* (Insomniac Press, 1996), *The Incredible Journey of the Instant Anthology* (Toronto Small Press Fair, 2001), *The Instant Anthology* (Toronto Small Press Book Fair, 1992), *The Instant Anthology* (Toronto Small Press Fair, 1998), *Jewel in the Lotus of the Instant Anthology* (Toronto Small Press Fair, 2000), *Loose Watch: A Lost and Found Times Anthology* (Invisible Books, 1998), *The Thing in Exile* (Books by Kids, 1975), *The WHIPlash 2 Reader* (above/ground press, 1997); in the books *Bad Glamour* (Proper Tales Press, 1980), *Bunnybaby: The Child with Magnificent Ears* (Proper Tales Press, 1988), *Farmer Gloomy's New Hybrid* (ECW Press, 1999), *In This World* (Silver Birch Press, 1992), *The Inspiration Cha-Cha* (ECW Press, 1996), *Ladies & Gentlemen, Mr. Ron Padgett* (Proper Tales Press, 1989), *Little Black Train* (Proper Tales Press, 1993), *Paralysis Beach* (Pink Dog Press, 1988), *Poodle* (Proper Tales Press, 2001), *Razovsky at Peace* (ECW Press, 2001), *Runts* (Proper Tales Press, 1992), *The Shopping Mall* (Proper Tales Press, 1996), *Sitting by the Judas Hole* (Proper Tales Press, 1998), *Skip & Biff Cling to the Radio* (Proper Tales Press, 1984), *When Electrical Sockets Walked Like Men* (Proper Tales Press, 1981); and in leaflet, postcard, T-shirt, or poster form from above/ground press, Bathrooms & Elevators, Curvd H&z, Flying Camel, 1cent, Proper Tales Press. "Three Scoops, Waffle Cone" appeared as part of the Toronto Transit Commission's Poetry on the Way campaign in 2001; "Do Not Ask Where I Started" was commissioned by CBC Radio One for the 2003 National Poetry Face-Off.

Big thanks to publisher Jack David for the lightbulb and editor Michael Holmes for the arm-wrestling, and to the rest of the gang at ECW. I'm grateful for valuable, thoughtful feedback on this project from Kevin Connolly, jwcurry, Elyse Friedman, Richard Huttel, Lance La Rocque, and Dana Samuel. Toronto's amazing small press community has challenged and inspired me.

Many of these poems were triggered by or written for friends who know — the love and/or debt is archived in my gut.